PENGUIN BOOKS

HOLDING OUR WORLD TOGETHER

Brenda J. Child, a member of the Red Lake Ojibwe Nation, is an associate professor of American Studies at the University of Minnesota and the author of *Boarding School Seasons: American Indian Families, 1900–1940.*

HOLDING OUR WORLD TOGETHER

TOGETHER

*Ojibwe Women
and the
Survival of Community*

BRENDA J. CHILD

THE PENGUIN LIBRARY
OF AMERICAN INDIAN HISTORY

PENGUIN BOOKS

PENGUIN BOOKS

Published by the Penguin Group

Penguin Group (USA) Inc., 375 Hudson Street, New York, New York 10014, U.S.A.

Penguin Group (Canada), 90 Eglinton Avenue East, Suite 700, Toronto, Ontario M4P 2Y3, Canada
(a division of Pearson Penguin Canada Inc.)

Penguin Books Ltd, 80 Strand, London WC2R 0RL, England

Penguin Ireland, 25 St Stephen's Green, Dublin 2, Ireland (a division of Penguin Books Ltd)

Penguin Group (Australia), 707 Collins Street, Melbourne, Victoria 3008, Australia
(a division of Pearson Australia Group Pty Ltd)

Penguin Books India Pvt Ltd, 11 Community Centre, Panchsheel Park, New Delhi–110 017, India

Penguin Group (NZ), 67 Apollo Drive, Rosedale, Auckland 0632, New Zealand (a division of Pearson
New Zealand Ltd)

Penguin Books (South Africa), Rosebank Office Park, 181 Jan Smuts Avenue, Parktown North 2193, South Africa

Penguin China, B7 Jiaming Center, 27 East Third Ring Road North, Chaoyang District, Beijing 100020, China

Penguin Books Ltd, Registered Offices: 80 Strand, London WC2R 0RL, England

First published in the United States of America by Viking Penguin,
a member of Penguin Group (USA) Inc. 2012
Published in Penguin Books 2013

1 3 5 7 9 10 8 6 4 2

THE LIBRARY OF CONGRESS HAS CATALOGED THE HARDCOVER EDITION AS FOLLOWS:
Child, Brenda J., 1959–
Holding our world together : Ojibwe women and the survival of community / Brenda J. Child.
p. cm. — (Penguin library of American Indian history)
Includes bibliographical references and index.
ISBN 978-0-670-02324-0 (hc.)
ISBN 978-0-14-312159-6 (pbk.)
1. Ojibwa women—History. 2. Ojibwa women—Social conditions. 3. Ojibwa women—
Economic conditions. I. Title. E99.C6C48 2011 977.004'97333—dc23 2011036175

Printed in the United States of America
Set in Granjon LT Std

While the author has made every effort to provide accurate telephone numbers, Internet addresses, and other
contact information at the time of publication, neither the publisher nor the author assumes any responsibility for
errors or for changes that occur after publication. Further, the publisher does not have any control over and does
not assume any responsibility for author or third-party Web sites or their content.

To Benay Jeanette,
and her generation of
jingle dress dancers

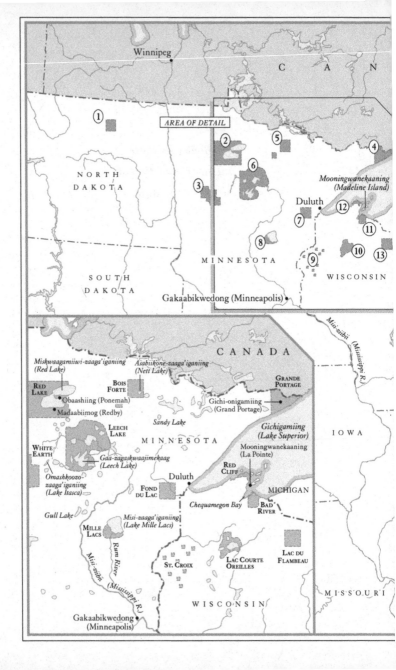

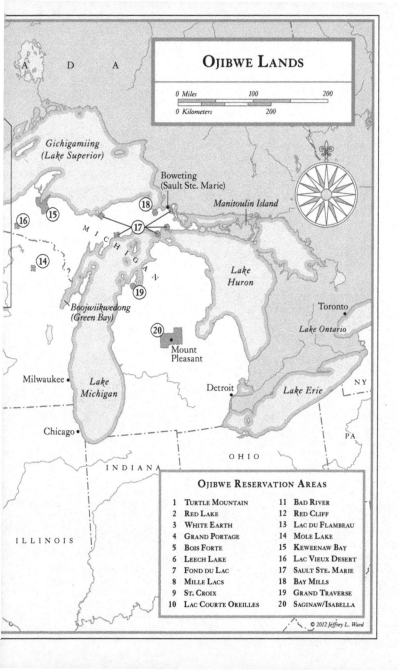

OJIBWE LANDS

0 Miles 100 200
0 Kilometers 200

Gichigamiing
(Lake Superior)

Boweting
(Sault Ste. Marie)

Manitoulin Island

MICHIGAN

(18)

(15)

(16)

(17)

(14)

Lake Huron

(19)

Boojwiikwedong
(Green Bay)

Toronto

(20)

Lake Ontario

Mount Pleasant

Milwaukee •

Lake Michigan

Detroit •

Lake Erie

NY

Chicago •

PA

OHIO

INDIANA

ILLINOIS

OJIBWE RESERVATION AREAS

1	TURTLE MOUNTAIN	11	BAD RIVER
2	RED LAKE	12	RED CLIFF
3	WHITE EARTH	13	LAC DU FLAMBEAU
4	GRAND PORTAGE	14	MOLE LAKE
5	BOIS FORTE	15	KEWEENAW BAY
6	LEECH LAKE	16	LAC VIEUX DESERT
7	FOND DU LAC	17	SAULT STE. MARIE
8	MILLE LACS	18	BAY MILLS
9	ST. CROIX	19	GRAND TRAVERSE
10	LAC COURTE OREILLES	20	SAGINAW/ISABELLA

© 2012 Jeffrey L. Ward

CONTENTS

❆

INTRODUCTION

Maps of Birch Bark

OJIBWE COMMUNITIES in the United States and Canada are linked historically through kinship, language, culture, politics, and identity. They also share a memory of a time many generations ago when their Anishinaabeg ancestors migrated from the St. Lawrence River to the Straits of Mackinac, a narrow waterway that connects Lake Huron and Lake Michigan, separating Michigan's Upper and Lower Peninsulas. Maps of birch bark preserved their migration stories. Michilimackinac (the "Great Turtle"), an island in the straits with a prominent mounded form, was famous for the pike, sturgeon, and whitefish that swam in the cold, blue waters, and it remained for many years the nucleus of the Great Lakes Indian world. Michilimackinac proved to be a momentous place in the Anishinaabeg's journey to their homelands, for it was here that the Ojibwe parted from their relatives, the Potawatomi and the Ottawa. The Ojibwe settled at Boweting, the outlet of Gichigamiing (Lake Superior) later referred to by French settlers as Sault Ste. Marie. In the early seventeenth century, a portion of the Boweting population moved west to form a significant southern Ojibwe settlement that became known after the fur trade as the village of La Pointe, on Lake Superior's Madeline Island, in present-day Wisconsin's

Chequamegon Bay. Today a common identity as Anishinaabeg endures for the Potawatomi, Ottawa, and Ojibwe peoples, even though their division took place in the sixteenth century.[1]

After their historic journey up the waterways of the Great Lakes around the time of Columbus, Ojibwe clans found economic opportunity and resources that allowed them to spread over a vast region of central North America, constructing communities that by the middle of the eighteenth century were located north of Lake Ontario, around Lake Huron and Georgian Bay, and north of Lake Michigan. The Ojibwe settled on all sides of Lake Superior and as far west as Red Lake, in present-day Minnesota. Ojibwe people who lived near the Minnesota headwaters of one great river named it the Misi-ziibii, or Mississippi. Anishinaabewaki, or Ojibwe territory, spanned both sides of an international border being defined in the aftermath of the American Revolution, a delineation that initially had little consequence for the Ojibwe. They and neighboring nations inhabited a landscape encompassing the Great Lakes as well as the surrounding land and the waters that flow into them; rivers and lakes formed the main roads on the map of Anishinaabewaki.

This book is a history of Ojibwe community life in the Great Lakes since the early nineteenth century, one that unites historical sources featuring the words and experiences of generations of Ojibwe women, especially near Gichigamiing and the Mississippi, where a gendered economy founded on wild rice flourished. The Ojibwe entry into the wild rice district was a milestone marking the end of a journey. With the renewal of community life in the western Great Lakes, Ojibwe women began to hold an important and unique place in their cultures. They inhabited a world in which the earth was gendered female, and they played powerful roles as healers. They organized labor within their community and held property rights over water, making decisions and controlling an essential part of the seasonal economy. Ojibwe women lived in a society that valued an entire system of beliefs associated with women's work, not just the product of their labor.

When Europeans settled in the Great Lakes, and with the beginning of the fur trade economy in the eighteenth century, Indian women were often positioned as political, social, and economic intermediaries between their people and the newcomers. Women married traders, bridged cultures, and worked to resolve disputes, ensuring sustenance and survival for both their people and the Europeans in an era increasingly complicated by the demands of Western intrusion. Indian women's lives grew ever more complex during the removal and reservation years, when indigenous political and cultural sovereignty were being undermined by the authority of the U.S. government and Christian organizations. For the Ojibwe, colonial violence against people and the land during the reservation and assimilation era, which began in the nineteenth century, put in jeopardy their traditional economy. This had many repercussions for Ojibwe society, and men and women began to negotiate new labor roles within their communities.

Remarkably, there may be more of a consensus among historians regarding the status of Indian women during the fur trade era than in more recent decades. We are only now beginning to grasp the nature of women's lives in the twentieth century, especially as more than half of the American Indian population moved to cities in the decades before and after World War Two. My own interviews with Ojibwe women in Minneapolis suggest that women did not forsake the values associated with traditional forms of labor but, rather, found ways to infuse the principles associated with the wild rice economy into urban community living. For the past two centuries in their homeland, Ojibwe women seem to have been working against the weight of history as they sought to control their own destinies. The extension of American colonialism, relocation and reservations, dispossession, and the decline of their traditional economy all presented countless problems for the Ojibwe and their society, yet women's efforts on behalf of their communities have not significantly diminished.

Getting a clear picture of gender roles in American Indian history has long been a challenge. Early generations of historians lacked the tools and perspective to put them in context. Also, historical sources and documents often misunderstood and misrepresented the Ojibwe and other peoples, portraying women with great contempt or trivializing their work and moral character. Nonetheless, the historical archive—even one produced by biased men who were colonizing North America—can shed light on the history of Ojibwe women in the Great Lakes, especially when colonial documents can be put side by side with Ojibwe accounts of the past. English literacy also became more common among Indian peoples after the arrival of missionaries and the advent of the government boarding school, and Ojibwe writers have left fascinating accounts.

American historians have usually written about the Ojibwe from the perspective of politics. Among the more than one thousand federally recognized tribal nations in the United States and Canada today, the Ojibwe view their political organizations as small nations, with historic political ties to the Ottawa and Potawatomi. After their separation from the Ottawa and the Potawatomi at Michilimackinac, the Ojibwe remained part of an Anishinaabeg political confederacy, the Council of the Three Fires. One widely held view about the name Ojibwe is that it relates to the practice of writing down information and sacred songs in drawings and glyphs on birch bark, from the root *ozhibii'*. It was the Ojibwe ceremonial responsibility within the council to maintain these birch bark scrolls. Another popular interpretation with linguistic veracity is that Ojibwe refers to a kind of puckered moccasin. Within their own communities, Ojibwe, Ottawa, and Potawatomi refer to themselves as Anishinaabeg, a highly evocative term that originates in sacred stories and holds a stronger spiritual association. To be Anishinaabe is to be human.

In treaty negotiations and later in describing federal and state relationships, the U.S. government often referred to the Anishinaabeg as Chippewa. That term has endured, though most Ojibwe find it linguistically inaccurate. In addition to the Potawatomi and the Ottawa, the Ojibwe are related to other Algonquian speakers. Anishinaabemowin, their rich and descriptive language, has more than a dozen dialects and is historically (and currently) one of the most prevalent indigenous languages in North America. In the Great Lakes, where indigenous people often spoke more than one language, knowledge of the Ojibwe language was extraordinarily useful, an advantage not missed by the population of early European traders and settlers.[2]

Ojibwe stories of westward migration from the lower St. Lawrence River were already old when French explorers, missionaries, and traders arrived in the Great Lakes, a time and place described as a middle ground of cultural negotiation.[3] Richard White, writing about the early encounters between Indians and Europeans in the region, described French Canada as a historical space where a balance of power existed and was maintained by distinct peoples through mediation and based on each group's mutual needs. Violence was part of the middle ground. In the second half of the seventeenth century, a period of instability and intermittent warfare began for the Ojibwe and other French-allied Great Lakes Indians as they became caught up in the Iroquois Wars, a military campaign to stop the western Indian fur trade. These took place as far west as northern Lake Michigan and eastern Lake Superior. After 1680, the Ojibwe and their allies successfully countered Iroquois attacks with their own expeditions along the water routes of Lake Ontario, finally forcing the Haudenosaunee, or Iroquois Confederacy, to defend their villages. In 1701, the Haudenosaunee negotiated the Great Peace of Montreal with the Ojibwe and other French-allied tribal nations, after which northern Ojibwe spread out from Georgian Bay to settle land between Lakes Huron, Erie, and Ontario. From 1720 until the British military victory at Montreal in 1760, the French dominated the fur trade with tribal nations in the Great Lakes region.

Throughout these same years, the Ojibwe expanded their territory in the Great Lakes, founding new communities east of Lake Superior but coming into conflict with the Dakota in the contested transition zone, a verdant region connecting the woodlands and prairie where white-tailed deer and wild rice were abundant. Historian Michael Witgen has described the Ojibwe and the Dakota as "two of the largest, most successful and politically diverse Native social formations to dominate the western interior" of North America; he further emphasizes that "both peoples held on to their land base until the second half of the nineteenth century, and both still maintain communities in these homelands."[4] Ojibwe narratives describe a major turning point at mid-century, with the tribe's success in the battle of Kathio in 1750; in the aftermath, the Dakota retreated to the Minnesota River, abandoning Mille Lacs, Sandy Lake, and other regions in central Minnesota as far north as Canada. Relations between the Ojibwe and the Dakota remained troubled for another century, with periods of sporadic violence and interludes of peace.[5] The Dakota writer Charles A. Eastman, in a discussion of Ojibwe-Dakota relations, considered it important to remember that "peaceful meetings were held every summer, at which representatives of the two tribes would recount to another all the events that had come to pass during the preceding year."[6]

The Ojibwe did not engage in warfare against the U.S. military, aside from their victories at the Straits of Mackinac in the War of 1812 and in a small conflict on the Leech Lake Reservation in 1898. They maintained relationships of trade and diplomacy and generally accommodated their new neighbors. Nonetheless, local, state, and federal authorities pressured them to negotiate treaties and surrender extensive areas of their homelands, sometimes falsely claiming Ojibwe hostility. In the most difficult times, Ojibwe leaders approached political dialogue with great dignity; as impressive representatives for their people, they negotiated for boundaries and hunting, fishing, and gathering rights over lands ceded in treaties while being tolerant of newcomers in their homelands who respected Ojibwe sovereignty.

Indians' removal from their homelands is generally associated with policies of the U.S. government in the 1830s, when southeastern tribes were forced to relocate to the Indian Territory of Oklahoma; but British Canada also experimented with Indian removal in the same era, after initiating a "civilization" program that called for Christian conversion. Ottawa and Ojibwe on the islands surrounding the north shore of Lake Huron were expected to consolidate in 1838 at Manitowaning, a settlement on rocky Manitoulin Island. Similar to removal plans in the United States, this was a strategy to open a large part of Upper Canada to Euro-Canadian settlement. Many Ojibwe resisted and eventually abandoned Manitowaning.[7] U.S. officials also planned Ojibwe removal from Michigan and Wisconsin at mid-century, imagining an Indian Territory in the north. One little-known genocidal event in the U.S. government's removal schemes took the lives of an estimated 12 percent of the Wisconsin Ojibwe population: promising annuity payments, authorities pressed the Ojibwe to travel hundreds of miles from home in early winter, to Sandy Lake, in Minnesota Territory, where they were trapped for six weeks of starvation and illness when food and annuities failed to arrive.[8]

During the years when the Ojibwe expanded their territory in the Great Lakes, the overall North American Indian population experienced a devastating decline, which did not subside until the last decade of the nineteenth century. It is estimated that the Great Lakes Indian population in the mid-eighteenth century numbered sixty thousand people of two dozen or more indigenous nations. By that time, European settlement and the effects of colonialism were already deadly for indigenous Americans, who encountered warfare, geographic removal, land loss, the destruction of their natural resources, environmental degradation, and—most lethal of all—the introduction of new pathogens causing highly trans-mittable diseases, such as smallpox. It is difficult to locate exactly when the first smallpox epidemic arrived in Anishinaabewaki, but numerous outbreaks are documented. William Whipple Warren, a significant nineteenth-century Ojibwe historian who also had European ancestry, commented on Ojibwe narratives regarding a major smallpox epidemic in the Great Lakes that raged from 1780 to 1782.[9] Eastern Michigan Ojibwe ceded Saginaw Valley reservation lands after a smallpox epidemic in 1837 ravaged their population. The Lake Superior Ojibwe reached a population nadir in 1900, a full decade after historical demographers suggest the general U.S. Indian population reached an all-time low. Even as smallpox sub-sided as a serious threat, diseases related to poor nutrition and diet, especially tuberculosis, became a scourge during the reservation era. The years since 1900 have been a time of modest population recovery for the Ojibwe in the United States and Canada, and their numbers have grown steadily since World War Two.[10]

Ojibwe leaders from Canada and the United States participated in treaties when confronted with westward settlement, and the treaties were made between governments. The first Canadian treaty was negotiated in southern Manitoba in 1871, a time when the United States began to refer to the treaty process with Indian nations as "agreements," while both treaties and agreements continued in full force under the law. The 1871 negotiation, known as Treaty 1, verbally confirmed to the Ojibwe their right to hunt and fish over the land being transferred. In 1873, indigenous leaders insisted on including provisions for hunting and fishing in Treaty 3, which involved shared responsibility over fifty-five thousand square miles, primarily in Ontario. Ojibwe leaders in the United States were also concerned about their continued right to hunt, fish, and gather over lands ceded to the federal government in nineteenth-century treaties, understanding that their livelihoods would be severely curtailed without those conditions. The Treaty of 1837 with the United States included terms that guaranteed this privilege, though Lake Superior Ojibwe leaders sold nearly nine thousand square miles of land in the agreement; it was not a removal treaty.[11] Ojibwe leaders negotiated treaties on behalf of their people in order to maintain the rights to use their land and to harvest and take responsibility for its resources while conceding that they would share their country with newcomers, many of whom were primarily interested in pine lands for lumbering.

Later Ojibwe migrations in the Great Lakes, a number of them involuntary, came in the aftermath of piecemeal negotiations in the United States and Canada, which resulted in Ojibwe holding on to a fraction of their extensive former territories in Michigan, Wisconsin, Minnesota, Ontario, and Manitoba. Reservations were established for the Lake Superior Ojibwe in 1854 in a historic negotiation with the United States, the Treaty of La Pointe. This treaty created four Wisconsin reservations, at Red Cliff, Bad River, Lac du Flambeau, and Lac Courte Oreilles; St. Croix and Mole Lake Ojibwe were left out of the treaty, without firm title to land until the twentieth century. Grand Portage, Fond du Lac, and Bois Forte Ojibwe were also designated as Lake Superior Chippewa and established Minnesota reservations. The Treaty of La Pointe and the Detroit Treaty of 1855 also created reservations in Michigan. The 1855 Treaty of Washington led to the establishment of northern Minnesota reservations, and an 1867 treaty created a large reservation, White Earth, intended as a new homeland for all the Minnesota Ojibwe, a plan only partially realized. Red Lake established reservation boundaries through an agreement negotiated in 1889. Ojibwe also founded new communities on the plains—one in the Turtle Mountains of North Dakota and another when the Little Shell Band moved into Montana—while others joined the Cree at Rocky Boy's in Montana.

A new chapter in the history of the Great Lakes emerged once territories, states, and provinces were founded in Anishinaabewaki. The early years were sometimes characterized by a rich encounter involving coexistence, intermarriage, commerce, and cultural exchange, in addition to conflict and violence. The always unsteady equilibrium ended once local and state governments established regional jurisdictions that attempted to intervene and challenge the rights reserved in treaties between indigenous nations and the federal government. Ojibwe living within the borders of new states, including Wisconsin and Minnesota, were steadily and systematically harassed for more than a century by citizens and local law authorities when they exercised treaty rights by hunting, fishing, and gathering in their homelands.

When the United States passed the Dawes General Allotment Act of 1887, calling for individual property ownership on reservations, a collection of circumstances opened the floodgates to land loss for Ojibwe and other American Indians. In the late nineteenth century, reformers and policymakers promoted allotment, which would break up traditional forms of land tenure, as the all-round solution to the "Indian problem." As in the prior removal and reservation-consolidation efforts of the U.S. government, land was identified as key to moving forward with a progressive Indian policy. Politicians and their allies reasoned that Indians must be "civilized" for their own advantage, become "Americanized" enough to be citizens of the United States, and turn into private property owners. There was a corresponding residential school system established in Canada and the United States, to instill values of individualism and assimilation in indigenous children. For many decades, thousands of young Indians were taken from their families to distant boarding schools designed to separate them from their identity and communities. Reservations, including White Earth, were plundered for land and resources by timber companies and their allies in business and politics during this era. Not until the 1930s did the United States abandon the policies of assimilation and allotment or begin to promote integration in public schools for American Indian children.

The dispossession of the allotment era led to an early-twentieth-century migration of American Indians to cities like Milwaukee, Chicago, Minneapolis, and St. Paul. The Twin Cities metropolitan area eventually became home to a population of thirty thousand from more than forty tribal nations. Ojibwe and other First Nations people have made Winnipeg and Toronto centers of their urban life, and other Canadian cities have sizable indigenous populations. World War Two gave further momentum to a migration already ignited by land loss and economic necessity. In another form of twentieth-century mobility, Ojibwe soldiers traveled to every theater of global conflict during the war. Indeed, native participation was higher than that of any other ethnic group or segment of the general population in the United States and Canada.

Minneapolis became the center of a national Indian activism in the late 1960s, when the American Indian Movement formed to combat police brutality and discrimination. The movement rapidly spread to other cities in the United States and Canada. There are today more than a thousand federally recognized First Nations governments and sovereign Indian tribes in Canada and the United States, and among those are a total Ojibwe population of more than 200,000, with 105,907 self-identified as Ojibwe in the United States and 94,350 in Canada.[12] The urban community has played a dynamic role in Indian life, yet most tribal people have remained fully engaged with family, culture, politics, and issues on reservations outside the city. In fact, the growth of Indian-owned businesses since the 1988 Indian Gaming Regulatory Act, with its employment opportunities on the reservations, led to a new migration of urban Indians back home. *Bryan v. Itasca County*, a court case initiated by tribal member Russell Bryan on the Leech Lake Reservation in Minnesota, led to the milestone U.S. Supreme Court decision in the 1970s that provided the legal foundation for Indian gaming. Bryan, who lived in a modest mobile home on Leech Lake, refused to pay the $147.95 tax on the trailer that Itasca County had levied, successfully challenging the long-standing practice of state regulation of tribes and tribal members on reservation land without the approval of Congress.[13] Ojibwe people, who still hold considerable real estate in the United States and maintain dozens of communities in Canada, are political partners in the protection of sovereignty in their nations, which are primarily located in the provinces of Ontario and Manitoba and the states of Michigan, Wisconsin, Minnesota, North Dakota, and Montana.

. . .

My own Ojibwe community is the Red Lake Reservation, in northern Minnesota, the place where I was born and hold tribal membership. In area, Red Lake is the largest Ojibwe place in the United States or Canada completely owned by its original people. Our landscape encompasses more than eight hundred thousand acres of forest, land, and water, including one of the largest freshwater lakes in the United States and dozens of smaller lakes and wetlands. I come from an extraordinarily strong community with a powerful sense of place and a commitment to interpreting and remembering history. History is deeply rooted in our family stories and community life. We are the descendants of earlier generations who were deeply affected by treaties and land and assimilation policies, and because of that we have a profound awareness of our survival as a people. My earlier book, *Boarding School Seasons: American Indian Families, 1900–1940,* was motivated and influenced by the experiences of my grandmother Jeanette Jones Auginash, who, as a young woman in the early 1920s, left Red Lake for a few years to attend a government boarding school in South Dakota.[14] My grandmother and her family spoke the Ojibwe language. When she returned home after her time at school to marry and raise five children, she and my grandfather also spoke Ojibwe with their children, who learned English as well once they began attending school on the reservation. The youngest of their children was my mother, Florence Auginash Child. My mother, aunts, and uncles taught us about their experiences growing up on the reservation before and after World War Two. My uncles were veterans of the Korean War and had great, raucous stories of their time away from Red Lake when they were young men. They liked to hunt, trap, and fish—and tell stories about hunting and trapping and fishing at Red Lake.

I now realize that my grandmother, mother, and aunts had different memories of Red Lake. They frequently talked about the seasonal cycle they enjoyed as Ojibwe people, the wild-rice camp they set up in August, running from bears while picking blueberries, working the sugar bush, and making holes in the ice in winter to retrieve fresh water. One of the defining stories of my mother's childhood involved her family's annual pilgrimage to visit Bizhik, a medicine woman of some prominence who lived in Ponemah, a small Ojibwe town that rises from the water on a peninsula where our vast freshwater lake divides into lower and upper portions. As they do today, our family lived in Redby, some twenty miles south around the other side of the lake. I grew up understanding that women figured prominently in Ojibwe families and communities and witnessing the tragedy of social problems and poverty. The elders were always a source of strength. We respected women who assumed demanding economic and cultural roles, and we deferred to a power and authority that seemed to grow even more concentrated with age and maturity. My work as a historian has always been inspired by the Auginash family and the people of Red Lake, as well as by my experiences working in archives and teaching history and American Indian studies in the university.

Holding Our World Together: Ojibwe Women and the Survival of Community makes a case for the significant involvement of women as society builders, which allowed their communities to persevere in an era dominated by the expansion of American colonialism. At each stage, women marshaled much of the economy, and their roles and traditions were critical in sustaining Ojibwe communities in the face of forces that often aimed not only to cause physical destruction but to stamp out their entire way of life. Women like Nodinens, an Ojibwe from central Minnesota born in the nineteenth century who worked with the enthnologist Frances

Densmore, illustrate patterns of life that encompassed skill and environmental virtuosity in working the highly coordinated efficiency of the Ojibwe seasonal round, a lifestyle slated for obliteration and considered primitive in her own time.[15] Nodinens is one of dozens of women who have eloquently narrated a significant aspect of the Great Lakes region's history and, in the process, provided useful information that explains how Ojibwe people developed patterns of life that would one day help them survive the unpredictability and unemployment that came with reservations.

Spoken and written records have allowed me to research women in the twentieth century as allotment, changing family structures, education in boarding schools, relocation, and the influence of Christianity caused once resilient parts of Ojibwe life to weaken, posing a challenge to women's long-standing roles. Wars and military service, new policies after the wars, and economically depressed reservations compelled Indians to relocate to urban centers, where women committed to new agendas in the community. Women worked long and hard, but they could not counter all the effects of colonialism and federal policies that undermined Ojibwe sovereignty and community life. Ojibwe writer Gerald Vizenor, born in Minneapolis, frequently invokes the word *survivance* to describe the unique history of survival and resistance that sustained indigenous creativity within their communities, despite conditions of domination and colonialism. Like Wazhashk, the resilient muskrat whose fortitude defines the outcome of more than one indigenous creation story, the Ojibwe people have survived. In every journey and story of survivance, women were at the heart of the Ojibwe sense of their world.

After five centuries in the western Great Lakes, Ojibwe people keep alive a memory of that long historic journey that brought them to their homelands. For them, the community is a place but also a spiritual space that binds them together in a sacred landscape. The survival of that community has never been guaranteed, and as we will see, it came with a heavy price. Even today, our language and, with it, many aspects of our indigenous knowledge and culture continue to be endangered. It is therefore reassuring that many of our people still live close to the land and to history, allowing Ojibwe historical knowledge to remain dynamic and survive in stories and places. We gain insight into the past by living in and caring deeply about the same landscape that our ancestors did, singing songs they composed, or working as they did by fishing or harvesting wild rice. My goal has been to remember the work and vision of generations of Ojibwe women who shaped life in their communities, a force greater than treaties that binds us to our homelands.

HOLDING OUR WORLD
TOGETHER

1

WOMEN OF THE
GREAT LAKES AND MISSISSIPPI

Everything Was Very Systematic

❋

FOR CENTURIES, one of the dynamic centers of Ojibwe life has been the sprawling homeland that surrounds the gentle northern flow of the headwaters of the Mississippi River.[1] Historically, this was a highly sought-after indigenous social space, filled with bogs, wild rice, and giant pines, and it was contested by the two most significant military and economic powers in the western Great Lakes, the Ojibwe and the Dakota, the latter eventually being forced out. The homeland was also a ritual landscape. Ojibwe people referred to the lake at the headwaters as Omashkooz, or Elk, as they renamed the important bodies of water in the upper Mississippi, and became spiritual caretakers for burial mounds near the great river.[2] Leech Lake, one of the largest bodies of water in the upper Mississippi region, was a largely peaceful settlement of numerous autonomous Ojibwe communities that collectively formed a stronghold of Ojibwe power and politics in the century following the Dakota expulsion.

There is an impressive narrative from the early nineteenth

century about a young girl who grew to womanhood on the lake "where the giant leeches abound," one that illustrates some of the ways in which Ojibwe women exercised power in their communities. Bear Woman, who in early life was called Ne Zet, related the events to her grandchildren Ellen Bellanger and Edward Carl, but other Ojibwe people have also related parts of her heroic story.[3] Bellanger and Carl recalled their grandmother as being born in the early 1830s in a community that was located in what is today the Leech Lake Reservation.[4] During Ne Zet's childhood, the economic and territorial conflicts between the Ojibwe and the Dakota had greatly diminished, but small and sporadic episodes of violence took place through the mid-century.

Bear Woman's story is a singular and intimate portrayal of one girl's puberty experience, yet it also contains a broader societal interpretation of the lifelong value of the vision quest. Her coming-of-age story points to the responsibility deliberately placed on the shoulders of very young people and to the ways in which the various stages of the human life cycle were recognized as an occasion for encouraging all individuals to behave in socially responsible ways. Her narrative also gives us a picture of one Ojibwe family and community and the rich cycles of their seasonal economy, which included connections to a world of European trade.

> Their people had lived here for years. They were well known for their strength and bravery. It was a good place to live. They were used to the pattern of life here. There was travelling to the sugar camps in the springtime and the wonderful sugar cakes that her mother and grandmother made for her and all the children. These sugar cakes lasted all year, and in the cold of winter, they had the cakes to suck on while the story teller wove his bedtime stories. In the early springtime,

after the sugar camps, there were the great get togethers or rendezvous. Here is where all the news of the winter was exchanged. People came from all over. Feasts were held far into the night. Families chose future partners in life for their children following the clan rules. And the dancing, there was always the dancing. Everyone looked forward to these gatherings. One of the special things that came to the women of the village was the kettle. What a difference it made. It saved hours of work in the sugar camp and could be used for parching rice. Ne Zet always remembered the time her brother brought her a crimson ribbon for her pretty black hair. She saved it for special occasions.

Ojibwe girls spent many years mastering the skills necessary for family survival and prosperity in an apprenticeship that began early. By the time Ne Zet reached the age of eleven or twelve, she had already received an important part of her education from the women of her family. Her grandchildren remembered that she was also skilled at beadwork, preferring beads over porcupine quills. What is perhaps the most remarkable aspect of the survival of Bear Woman's story is that, so many years later, Bellanger and Carl would be able to describe in great detail their grandmother's puberty experience and the significance of her coming-of-age. Like many other North American Indian peoples, the Ojibwe instituted ceremonies to address the physical transition adolescents experience as their bodies and intellectual abilities mature. Indian people regarded this phase of the life span as especially critical.[5] Ne Zet's puberty was a crucial first stage of a significant physical and spiritual transformation, one that allowed her to achieve distinction and fulfillment as Bear Woman in later years. During her seclusion, Ne Zet had an empowering vision.[6]

She built a little house made of birch bark, just big enough for herself to stand, and waited within for something to happen. Her hair and hands were covered. She began her fast and vision quest. Day one passed quickly. On day two, she was beginning to feel hunger and thirst, although she was allowed a little water to drink. By day four, she began to feel weak and things became blurry. She fell into a deep sleep. Time was non-existent and she had no idea how long she slept. During this sleep, she had a vision of a great bear coming toward her. As it came closer, it got smaller in size, and when it was right beside her, she suddenly became the bear. She felt wonderful—powerful and strong. When she awoke, her mother and grandmother were beside her. They washed her warm face with cool water. They knew she had had her vision. They helped her up and together they all returned to the village. They said nothing about it but gave her time to consult with the elders who interpret the visions.

The elders told Ne Zet she would grow into a woman with "a strong heart and the courage of a bear." A feast was held with venison, wild rice, and other special food, to "celebrate her entry into the group as a young woman." Ne Zet grew up to be physically strong, married, and had children of her own. In the story that Bellanger, Carl, and other descendants heard all their lives, Ne Zet was with her family at Leech Lake when they were attacked by the Dakota. As her husband and other relatives were killed before her eyes Ne Zet remained courageous and strong, the bear of her vision, and saved the lives of her children. Memories of the battle include references to a fierce black bear fighting off the enemy.

The Leech Lake story of Bear Woman suggests that the power unique to females intensified and incorporated greater responsibility with the onset of puberty, when propriety was expected of young women entering a life stage recognized as sacred. Even very early observers of Ojibwe life noted that "none of the subsisting Indian customs are more significant than those connected with the menstrual lodge."[7] Ojibwe women were born into a society that valued their participation in the material and spiritual well-being of their community. Women were thought to hold an innate strength because of their life-giving ability, and girls began to be prepared at a young age for ceremonies that took place at first menstruation. Growing up, both male and female children were encouraged to consider the meanings of their dreams, perhaps in preparation for "the important dream, or vision, that was sought a few years later."[8] Fasting and seclusion from family and community were part of the female experience at puberty. This was a special time in a young woman's life that affirmed connections to her family, community, and *doodem*, or clan.[9]

Ojibwe women regarded this time as ideal for female mentoring. Mothers and grandmothers attended the girl during days of seclusion, advising and instructing her on developmental changes and societal responsibilities. Small tasks, such as sewing or beadwork, filled the girl's quiet days. As Bear Woman's experience suggests, the period of contemplation and rituals of the first menstruation concluded with a feast, during which guests were offered berries. The first menstruation was largely experienced with mothers and female relatives, though male relatives and singers were sometimes present. Strawberries were the preferred first food for the young woman being honored after the puberty fast. Strawberries hold such a strong association with the female gender and puberty traditions among the Ojibwe that the event is today often referred to as the Berry Fast.

Bear Woman's story supports the idea that spiritual power was believed to come to Ojibwe girls at the time of first menstruation. In some instances, as with Ne Zet, girls were also encouraged to fast and seek visions, though historical sources indicate that the vision quest was expected more consistently of boys.[10] The suspension of normal activities and isolation that characterized the female rite of passage was not in any way regarded as penance or punishment; rather, it was an occasion that affirmed, comforted, indeed even empowered young women at a moment of change and insecurity. At the same time, Ojibwe society had exceedingly high expectations for children and required a great deal of their young women, who would, in a few short years, fulfill an adult role with considerable family and community responsibility. Proper socialization and character development was essential to the well-being of the whole community.

Another rare and remarkably intimate recollection of a female coming-of-age was told to Ojibwe writer Jane Johnston Schoolcraft in the nineteenth century, who translated it from the original Ojibwe narrative. The extraordinary storyteller Catherine Wabose suggested that some mothers asked more of their daughters than seclusion, because of special issues related to the family or for spiritual reasons.

> When I was a girl of about twelve or thirteen years of age, my mother told me to look out for something that would happen to me. Accordingly, one morning early, in the middle of winter, I found an unusual sign, and ran off as far from the lodge as I could, and remained there until my mother came and found me out. She knew what was the matter, and brought me nearer to the family lodge, and bade me help her in making a small lodge of branches of the spruce tree. She told me to remain there, and keep away from everyone, and as a

diversion, to keep myself employed in chopping wood, and that she would bring me plenty of prepared basswood bark to twist into twine. She told me that she would come to see me in two days, and that, in the meantime, I must not even taste snow.[11]

Catherine Wabose remembered the intensity of what turned out to be a ten-day fast and isolation, during which only her mother visited her from time to time. On the sixth day she began to experience a vision of "a thin shining path, like a silver cord, which I followed." It led her to a spiritual being identified as Everlasting Standing Woman, who passed on to her powerful gifts, including "long life on the earth, and skill in saving life in others," and her spiritual name.[12]

A name that derived from a vision, especially in the course of coming-of-age rituals, was extraordinarily meaningful for a young man or woman. At other times, names were bestowed by an elder or a person with knowledge of medicines. Ojibwe people regarded naming as a reciprocal relationship, which created a spiritual bond between individuals that was different from a child's tie with parents, as embodied in the notion of the namesake, or *niiyawe'enh*. Like the experience of coming-of-age, names were spiritually empowering.

The year following the first menstruation was regarded as a special phase of an Ojibwe woman's life. This time was marked by some social prohibitions and often concluded with a short fast, followed again with the ritual eating of strawberries. The demanding rituals associated with puberty, which involved considerable time and commitment by the young woman and other female relatives, do not seem to have been primarily concerned with fertility. Instead, the rituals involved in the first menstruation represent a highly meaningful coming-of-age symbolizing a woman's power to give life that is first and foremost associated with the powers of the universe, and therefore linked to the rest of the community. Female rituals acknowledged the sacredness of life and the centrality of women's roles in society. The Ojibwe Berry Fast simultaneously celebrated tradition, the present life of a young woman, and the future.[13]

Nodinens, an Ojibwe woman from central Minnesota, offered a significant, albeit brief, narrative in which she described her mother's advice when she was growing up in the nineteenth century. Nodinens was told that "I must live a quiet life and be kind to all, especially the old, and listen to the advice of the old. She said that people would respect me if I did this and would be kind to me." Early accounts by explorers and settlers frequently described Indian women as licentious and immoral, but Ojibwe historical sources suggest that such behavior, if it actually occurred, stood in direct opposition to the advice older women handed down to daughters. Nodinens' mother advised her to be sensible and aware of her sexuality: "Do not run after a boy. If a young man wants to marry you, let him come here to see you and come here to live with you. This is the reason I am always telling you to be industrious and how to live, so that when you have a home of your own you will be industrious and do right to the people around you."[14] Young women of marriageable age were closely guided, supervised, and educated by the older women of their family, and women generally did not go far from home even after marriage, which encouraged strong ties to both kin groups and allowed them to care for and work with relatives.

Marriage did not hold the same significance in the Ojibwe female life cycle as in Western society, but Ojibwe people did marry, which they referred to as walking with another person. *Wiidige-maagan* was a gender-neutral term for *companion* and might refer to a husband or a wife. Ojibwe family life was constructed in a way that gave ultimate priority to the kin group of one's birth; the sibling relationship was especially strong, more influential in the long view of things than a marital partnership. After marriage an Ojibwe woman retained membership in her own *doodem*, or clan, though her children were considered part of the father's *doodem*. The Ojibwe clan system influenced Ojibwe ideas about marriage; individuals who carried the same *doodem* were forbidden to intermarry. Perhaps twenty clans existed among the Ojibwe people by the mid-nineteenth century; ostensibly this made marriage within the *doodem* easily avoidable, though most southeastern Ojibwe were members of the crane, catfish, bear, marten, wolf, or loon *doodem*.

Marriage bonds were strong but not necessarily irrevocable. Separation or divorce was an accepted practice when a couple could not get along; the wife simply returned to her kin group and often married again, as might her husband. Rituals associated with marriage and divorce also varied by time and region. Ojibwe elders interviewed during the 1930s in the Federal Writers' Project of the Works Progress Administration's oral history series explained the community's way of handling divorce and reconciliation, suggesting that both were "usually announced at a public dance or meeting." A blanket served as a symbol of the union and its dissolution. When a man sought to separate from a wife, after making "a public statement to the effect that he was dissolving his marriage, he tore the blanket in half, rolled it up and threw it outside. The other half he kept. The couple were then considered divorced." If a couple decided to reconcile, the husband might speak in public once again and make "amends by making gifts of clothing for the trouble he had caused, and the marriage, therefore, was reestablished and the woman reinstated as a wife."[15]

The community was the social body responsible for the public acknowledgment of marriage, divorce, and reconciliation, but the clan system also functioned to regulate marriage. The *doodem* passed down through the male line, and though residence patterns might be matrilocal, a more frequent practice was for women to join the family home of her husband.[16] As a consequence, Ojibwe families were often composed of brothers and their wives and off-spring, who enjoyed a close, siblinglike relationship and shared clan membership. Wives and husbands had different *doodem* and were not clan relatives, which allowed for flexibility in the kinship network and created the potential for a social world with great hospitality and political alliances across families and communities. This system of interconnected family groups with ties to an ancestral *doodem*, which had organized life in the Great Lakes for generations, was not as pivotal to day-to-day society once reservations were established, ushering in a new era of federal and regional authority over Ojibwe politics and where and how the Ojibwe would live.

Plural marriage was an accepted practice, associated more with the social, political, or economic stability of a kin group than with sexual indulgence or patriarchy. Later, during the reservation era, it became rare, discouraged by U.S. government officials and Christian clergy who viewed regulating indigenous marriage as a part of their mission of civilization. Therefore, it is ironic that the most famous story of an Ojibwe plural marriage during the nineteenth century was between a non-Indian Christian, Ellen McCarty, and the prominent Mississippi Ojibwe leader Bagone-giizhig.

Bagone-giizhig, or Hole in the Day the Younger, was a politically controversial figure for both the Ojibwe and the Americans and is remembered for his personal ambition during a tension-filled period when the Ojibwe faced considerable cultural change, political fracture, and removals.[17] Dakota writer Charles A. Eastman once noted that Bagone-giizhig had a reputation for being "especially popular with the ladies."[18] By all accounts, Bagone-giizhig was an exceptionally handsome man with plenty of charisma, in addition to an aptitude for diplomacy. Eastman interviewed Ojibwe people in Minnesota during the early twentieth century who remembered Bagone-giizhig and described him as "tall and symmetrically formed, with much grace of manner and natural refinement." He had a legendary status for "marrying the daughter of a chief in nearly every band" for political advancement.[19] The Ojibwe historian William W. Warren was a contemporary of Bagone-giizhig's, and his sister, Julia Warren Spears, recalled their close friendship. Even many years later, she carried an indelible memory of his stunning appearance—large braids and feathered headdress, a green blanket, beaded leggings and moccasins, a black broadcloth coat and vest, and a pink calico shirt—and recalled that he was "very fond of pink."[20]

During an age when American Indian delegations were a novelty in Washington and often photographed, Bagone-giizhig visited more than once to negotiate on behalf of the Mississippi Ojibwe. He attracted crowds. As Eastman described one trip to the capital, Bagone-giizhig met "a handsome young woman who asked through the interpreter if the chief would consent to an interview about his people, to aid her in a paper she had promised to prepare." Bagone-giizhig was familiar with the English language but not proficient; nonetheless, the woman, Ellen McCarty, was deeply attracted to him, ignoring "all racial biases and differences of language and custom" and following him back to Minneapolis. In Eastman's account of Bagone-giizhig's Euro-American wife, he contends that McCarty remained in the city to avoid the possibility of indignation from his Ojibwe wives and that she gave birth to a son, who was raised by a white family named Woodbury after her death at an early age. Eastman claimed to have met him some years later in Washington.[21] Julia Warren Spears' version of this story is different. In a short, handwritten history, "Reminiscences of a Short Story of the Chippewa Chief Hole in the Day," she suggests that at the time he was killed, Bagone-giizhig resided "with his lawful wife a white woman," presumably McCarty, and their "one son." She also mentions "six children by his Indian wives."[22]

A woman named Quikabanokwe, or Dawn Woman, also offered insight into the history of Ojibwe marriage during the nineteenth century.[23] She related the significant stories of her life, including two marriages and a period of widowhood, to her grandsons, who collaborated to reconstruct a narrative about their grandmother in 1938, two years before her passing. Dawn Woman was born on the shores of a lake in northeastern Wisconsin the Ojibwe called Minisinokwog and was approximately ninety-eight when her grandsons interviewed her.[24] She was born sometime in the middle of the nineteenth century; her brother Gotchijigijig, or Edge of the Sky, who was also known as John Scott, served as a soldier in the Northern Army in the U.S. Civil War and resided in the Ojibwe community at Pakwewang.[25] She was old enough to remember the annuity payments held on Madeline Island that began after the first Ojibwe treaties, and especially the "meeting of friends and relatives" and the festivity of the "dances and games" that accompanied these gatherings.

Dawn Woman married her first husband, Manegoneosh, or Marksman, when she was thirty years old. His family was originally from the Hayward, Wisconsin, region, but later resided near L'Anse, on the Upper Peninsula of Michigan. Together Dawn Woman and Marksman had three children. Her grandsons warmly described her as an elderly woman who still "enjoys life." She shared with them her happy memories of marriage to their grandfather, who had died a half century before and whom she clearly had respected.

Manegoneosh was a good husband and a kind father. His family was always well provided for by his labors. He was a canoe maker of note and was always able to sell the results of his work. With the assistance of Rain Cloud he built one of the first hewn-log houses in Odanah. This was approximately seventy years ago, and the building was looked upon by the other Indians as a luxurious dwelling. It is still standing on the banks of the Bad River.[26]

Their happiness would not last. Marksman became disabled after he injured his back rafting on the Bad River. Wishing that his family not be "inconvenienced by his illness and that his children might be free to enjoy their romp and play," he built and lived in "a bark lodge across the river" from the comfortable log home. Marksman passed away, and after his burial in the old cemetery in Odanah, Wisconsin, his relatives adhered to a practice valid in Ojibwe society when they came from Michigan to collect the children. Dawn Woman's grandsons reconstructed her story of this painful period:

> After his death his relatives from L'Anse offered to adopt one or all of the children. They reasoned that because of the loss of their father, whose earnings were the sole support of his family, his children would suffer for want of the necessaries of life; but their mother, Qui-ka-ba-no-kwe, refused to part with the children, and her unceasing vigilance for their welfare as well as her efforts for their support after the loss of their father is deserving of mention.[27]

With the help of her eldest child, who was only six or seven years old, Dawn Woman strove to support her family in the aftermath of her husband's death. Even though her "youngest was still strapped in the di-ki-na-gun, or cradle board," she harvested all the foods in their natural environment and kept her family together through the resourceful gathering of "edible roots, nuts, berries, maple sugar, and wild rice." Her grandsons' admiration for her comes to life in their description of Dawn Woman's labor in the wild cranberry harvest, as they drew attention to their grandmother's skill for combining berry picking and child care.

> While picking the wild cranberries which thrive in the field-like marshes, the canoe was dragged away from the water or channel and taken further into the marsh where the water was not more than three or four inches deep. After cautioning the children to remain in the canoe, the mother picked the berries within sight and sound of the children. The older children played and slept in the craft the whole day, occasionally partaking of the food and drink left for them by their mother who also left her berry picking to "see how they were" from time to time. The surplus of these wild crops such as rice, berries, and maple sugar was sold or bartered to the logging camps and to the traders in Odanah and Bay City, the oldest settlement of what is now Ashland, Wisconsin.[28]

Members of the Ojibwe community did not abandon this hard-working widow, who from time to time received donations of meat and fish. Ojibwe fishermen contributed sturgeon to Dawn Woman's small family; these fish were regarded as somewhat of a nuisance in those days, as they frequently got caught up in fishing nets but had little value on the market because of their abundance. Eventually, Dawn Woman ended the "double burden of mother and provider for the family" by marrying John Diver, a Fond du Lac Ojibwe.

One of the underpinnings of reservation life was that American Indians conform to Anglo-Christian ideas about the role of husband, wife, and the family. In Ojibwe society, men did not gain the right to direct a woman's life or resources after marriage, and she maintained her separate clan identity. During the American era in the Great Lakes, and with the establishment of reservations, the U.S. government unceasingly promoted notions of private property ownership and, eventually, the system of land allotment, which principally conceived of households as headed by men. During Dawn Woman's second marriage, she and her husband took an allotment of land at Bayfield because of her heritage as a Bad River Ojibwe woman.[29]

The Ojibwe institution of marriage changed during the nineteenth century as part of broader societal transformations related to the influence of Christianity, Euro-American culture, and federal authority. Marriage to non-Indians was a factor in the decline of plural marriage, as was the reservation system itself. Even so, well after the creation of reservations, it is impossible to overemphasize the primacy of the greater body of kin in defining Ojibwe family relationships. Women continuously worked and otherwise interacted with relatives, and the roles of daughter, sister, mother, and aunt were important mantles of responsibility.

Ojibwe people liked to represent cultural attitudes about significant life events, social relationships, and worldviews in stories. The role of women is frequently referenced in stories about Nanabozhoo, the part-man, part-spirit trickster figure who is ubiquitous in Ojibwe storytelling traditions. Nanabozhoo was raised by his grandmother Nokomis after his mother died in childbirth. In an age when a mother or infant could quickly die or become sick, childbirth was taken very seriously, and women with skill in midwifery or healing were sought after for their experience.

Childbirth was another stage of a woman's life when her power was most intense, and consequently she carefully avoided some foods while pregnant and used particular medicines. Many of the plants Ojibwe women gathered were exclusive to female health issues and wellness. Long after the creation of reservations and even when the Ojibwe were confined to smaller areas of land, the scholar Frances Densmore found that seventeen of the nearly two hundred plants people identified by their Ojibwe name were described as medicines for "female diseases." Ojibwe women relied on a number of plants to treat menstrual discomforts, pregnancy and childbirth issues, and menopause.[30] As the stories suggest, Nokomis had power to heal and wisdom regarding medicine, and knowledge of plants and their healing properties was especially valuable to the community.

One of the more special and exquisite forms of everyday material culture Ojibwe women created was the cradleboard, a simple wooden frame supporting an elaborately decorated cloth used for carrying children. Ojibwe stories of its origin refer to a young woman who gave birth to male twins who were *manidoog*, or spiritual beings. The new mother put the twins in cradleboards and carried them on her back so their feet did not touch the earth. As a consequence, the story explains, human infants do not walk at birth, unlike many newborns in the animal world.[31] For centuries, the cradleboard has been part of the first year of an Ojibwe childhood, though over time women adopted new materials in its construction, including glass beads and velvet fabric, to create innovative forms of decoration. Every observer of Ojibwe life took note of the cradleboard, or *dikinaagan*.[32] A baby in a cradleboard was special, and this notion was reflected in the language, which contained its own word to describe the arrangement, *dakobinaawaswaan*, "baby in a cradleboard," rather than simply *abinoojiiyens*, or "baby." Cradleboards were also highly functional, because they allowed women to perform other labor while carrying and attending a baby.

Florina Denomie was one of the Ojibwe writers who spoke with Ojibwe elders while working in the 1930s WPA project in Wisconsin, and she recorded how they cared for infants. They wrapped babies in blankets of buckskin lined with "fine white moss, which had previously undergone a thorough cleaning and drying," and a very fine, natural "Indian talcum powder" they processed that was far superior to the talcum "offered for sale by our modern drug stores." The cradleboard was designed for beauty and simplicity and served the needs of both mother and child. Denomie explained:

> When the baby was ten or more days old, it was placed in a "dikinagun" with moss packed around and under it, to insure a comfortable bed. At the head of the cradle board was a hoop-like attachment covered with beaded work. The baby was bound to this cradle with two strips of cloth of different designs, which had a meaning of some kind. This hoop attachment served three distinct purposes: first, as a frame for the support of a netting to protect the baby against flies, mosquitoes, and insects in the summer or for a blanket to protect it against the cold in winter; secondly, the hoop served as a convenient handle to move the cradle from place to place; thirdly, it protected the baby from getting hurt. Should the cradle board fall face downward, the hoop, since it was at the head end of it and the baby was strapped to the board, would ward off all possibility of harm. Aside from a good scare, the baby would be no worse off.[33]

Frequently constructed of linden or maple, the cradleboard's large wooden hoop circling the infant's head is where toys, beadwork, or other items, such as a dream catcher, dangled.[34] Stories associated with the dream catcher suggest that the web filtered out bad dreams and malevolence. The baby's swaddle, *dikineyaab*, was sometimes a simple wrapping, or it could be lavishly decorated by women with beadwork in floral and leaf patterns that were not only artful but alluded to the woodland ecosystem that gave rise to their creation. Ojibwe women found multiple uses for the birch, pine, oak, maple, and linden trees in their environment, and the wooden cradleboard illustrated how they interacted with the world around them.

When millions of trees were cut down in the nineteenth and twentieth centuries by timber companies exploiting the northern forests of the Great Lakes, women's relationship to the land was transformed; the decline of the cradleboard was a small symbol of this change. Early lumbering had the greatest impact on white pine forests; eventually old-growth hardwoods were harvested. With the destruction of the traditional resources, poverty, and the corresponding loss of some traditional arts on modern reservations, women made cradleboards less often, though babies still slept in a simple informal and popular infant swing made of folded blankets and rope. That Ojibwe women continued to make and design cradleboards for decades into the twentieth century suggests something about the boards' cultural value, not just their utility.

The female formative years and coming-of-age experience reinforced intergenerational ties. "The companionship of a Chippewa girl and her mother was very close and the child learned many household tasks by watching and helping her mother," noted Frances Densmore in the early twentieth century. "She was also taught to make maple sugar, gather wild rice, and do all a woman's tasks."[35]

Some of Densmore's finest ethnographic work was done in collaboration with Ojibwe women in the Great Lakes. She was entering a highly productive time in her career when she made her first trip to study Ojibwe life in the Mille Lacs community in 1907, having been born forty years before in Red Wing, Minnesota, 140 miles south of the reservation. She met a remarkable elder at Mille Lacs, Nodinens, who was seventy-four.

Nodinens was very articulate about the Ojibwe seasonal round and her own experience growing up, attributing any success in life to one fundamental principle: "I have tried to do as my mother taught me. . . . [A]t my age I look back and am so grateful to her for giving me this advice, and I think it is the reason I have been so blessed and prospered all my life."[36] Densmore learned that the education of young people was the duty of the family. She observed firsthand how various adults taught children through stories and oral tradition and by the example of their own work. Women performed an indispensable role in passing on cultural values and attitudes about labor across generations.

Over the course of the following two decades, Densmore intermittently collaborated with several dozen Ojibwe women from a number of reservations in the Great Lakes region, gaining insight into their attitudes about significant stages of the female life cycle, work, and worldview. In interviews with the oldest Ojibwe people she visited, she learned that these elderly women were granted considerable power and authority in their society. Her early-twentieth-century fieldwork coincided with a demand on the part of Minnesotans for more Ojibwe land, and Mille Lacs residents faced a shocking reality of violence and harassment, making it more remarkable that Densmore was able to witness the continuing cycle of Ojibwe life and the orderliness of male and female labor. She identified, documented, and collected for posterity the woodland tools associated with female work. She witnessed women's diverse skills and came to understand how women systematically relied on the varied resources within their environment to support their families and communities. Rather than a portrayal of Ojibwe life at its lowest ebb of the colonial tide, Densmore's ethnography, and the material culture she collected, is an unexpected story of how Ojibwe women continued to shape the world around them.[37]

According to Nodinens, her grandmother once "directed everything" related to household labor and female work sites, responsibilities that required sophisticated organizational skills to ensure Ojibwe survival. She told how Ojibwe women dried and stored large quantities of food to get through the long, cold season in the Great Lakes area. While her father hunted, her mother "put away the wild rice, maple sugar, and other food that we would need during the winter." After the ice began to freeze on Lake Mille Lacs, the family "started for the game field," their winter landscape among relatives. Entire families sometimes hunted their way north, moving toward the spring and summer work sites.[38] Nodinens recalled that her father might be absent with other men on longer hunting trips, sometimes not returning until after women had completed their spring labor.

The running of the maple sap was a welcome sign of spring for the Ojibwe. Another female work site was the sugar bush, where women annually returned and held usufruct rights to communal property. In the autumn, Ojibwe women cached food at the sugar bush work site, including wild rice and dried corn and fruits. Nodinens recalled one year traveling to the sugar bush in a snowstorm, prompting her father to improvise snowshoes for the older people in their group. When they arrived, the men went to ice fish while the women tapped the maple trees. Before the introduction of metal tools and kettles, Ojibwe women spent a day in the sugar bush gathering birch bark for buckets and spouts before tapping the trees, and moose hides became large reservoirs for the sap. Kettles purchased from traders were used to boil the clear, watery maple sap down to a sweet amber liquid; in an active sugar bush, the kettles boiled twenty-four hours a day. After thickening, the liquid was put in a trough, where women worked with paddles to make granulated maple sugar. Ojibwe women were very precise about the role of weather in the science of maple sugar cultivation. They understood that the best syrup resulted from years when the ground froze very deeply, with large snowfall accumulation. They favored the flavor and texture of the first run of sap, feeling that heavy rains in spring ruined the taste of syrup.

Nodinens remembered how elderly women organized labor and held things together in the sugar bush: "Grandmother had charge of all this, and made the young girls do the work."[39] Children delighted in maple snow cones and sugar candy, while adults liked hot coffee or tea made from the clear maple water. Fresh fish, served with sauces of dried cranberries and blueberries cooked and sweetened with the new maple syrup, was a relished meal in the sugar bush. Throughout the year, maple sugar seasoned wild rice, vegetables, corn, berries, fish, and meat. Cold water sweetened with maple sugar was a simple beverage.

Generations of women were expert at crafting a generously proportioned *makak*, a birch-bark container used for storing sugar and other food. Birch bark served many functions for women, because it could hold and boil liquids without degrading. Even in the twentieth century, Ojibwe women still preferred the simplicity and functionality of birch-bark taps rather than manufactured taps for maple trees long after they had switched to metal kettles for cooking. A large sugar bush might have as many as two thousand taps, yielding hundreds of gallons of syrup and similar quantities of sugar. Nodinens remarked on the thick syrup Ojibwe people referred to as the "last run of sap," which, along with fish, sustained families as they began setting up their summer gardens.[40]

North American Indian agriculture was frequently underestimated and underreported in European and American historical documents and writing, which devalued native peoples' social arrangement and portrayed them as wandering hunters incompetent about land use and private property. Many of these accounts were used to support American interests in appropriating Indian land for themselves. Indigenous agricultural practices were denigrated because women were the main farmers in nations like the Cherokee and others in the Southeast and the Iroquois in the Northeast, which upset European and American sensibilities of the proper sexual division of labor. Historians believe that indigenous agriculture has also been taken too lightly in the Great Lakes region. Early settlers and officials gave the false impression that the Anishinaabeg, including the Potawatomi around Lake Michigan, tended only small gardens for their immediate household use, rather than large agricultural fields that sustained the community.[41] Even though the growing season in the northernmost areas of the Great Lakes region was transitory, that did not prevent Ojibwe families from congregating near the lakeshores in summer houses, where they planted gardens of squash, pumpkins, and corn, expanding the variety of vegetables in the years after the fur trade, when potatoes also became a principal crop.

WPA writer Jerome Arbuckle, Dawn Woman's grandson, commented on how hard Ojibwe women of his grandmother's generation worked, through which they "developed great physical strength and ability." Dawn Woman remembered the role of Ojibwe agriculture in the nineteenth century and how women preserved food:

The corn was braided by the husks into long bunches which were hung from the rafters, to be used during the winter for hominy, which was prepared by the mother, who employed the old Indian method in the preparation. The beans were thrashed by hand, sacked and stored in a dry place. The pumpkins were cut into thin strips and dehydrated, put into containers and suspended from the rafters. A sufficient amount of potatoes for the winter was stored in the cabin, the balance was stored in pits which were from four to six feet in depth and lined and covered with straw or chaff and further covered with a mound of earth. These potatoes were dug up in the spring to replenish the scanty supply, and to be used for seed.[42]

Historically Ojibwe gardens developed in microclimates where water along the Lake of the Woods and Rainy River worked to prevent early frost. These sites comprised a fertile belt of islands where corn had been planted for generations beyond memory. Though nineteenth-century rhetoric downplayed the prevalence of indigenous agriculture in an attempt to bring Indians into line with Western ideas about yeoman farming, in fact, it was Ojibwe farmers who sold seed potatoes to the new European settlers arriving in Anishinaabewaki. This was at a time when Canadian officials remarked on "magnificent" Ojibwe fields of potatoes and corn. The Ojibwe and other Anishinaabeg in the Great Lakes region may have farmed even more during the years of the fur trade, because their surplus could be used in the market as women sold and exchanged food and supplies to fur traders and lumbermen.

Microhabitats produced small fruits that were a priority to Ojibwe women. Gathering strawberries, gooseberries, blueberries, raspberries, low- and high-bush cranberries, and other ground vegetation was another significant summer economic activity essential to year-round nutrition and survival, since these foods could be easily dried and stored. As important as berries were to Ojibwe subsistence, stories associated with certain plants always gave priority to their life-giving and spiritual essence over their nourishment. Berry season was such an essential and pleasant time for Ojibwe families and communities that summer months were named after the berries that ripen within those days. The heart berry, *ode'imin*, or strawberry was first to mature, and many Ojibwe identified June as the heart berry moon for its shape. Depending on the area of the Great Lakes region, July or August was considered *miinikegiziis*, the blueberry moon. Surplus fruits were increasingly a source of income, because they could be sold or bartered to traders, lumbermen, and settlers who arrived in Anishinaabewaki.

One early lumberman in central Minnesota was impressed by the sheer extent of wild rice–related labor taking place as he passed through six miles of lake where women had bound the crop before harvesting, forcing him to take his canoe ashore.[43] Prior to harvest, women went out to the rice lakes in small canoes and tied the stalks into sheaves with strips of basswood fiber, marking their territory, protecting the crop from high winds and birds, and creating paths for canoes. Indigenous people have harvested wild rice for a thousand years or more in the Great Lakes region, where it grows naturally in gentle, mineral-rich lakes and river headwaters. Ojibwe people called wild rice *manoomin*, "the good seed that grows in water," and the seasonal grain was sacred food as well as a dietary staple. The work of harvest began early in the spring with the selection of the Oshkaabewisag, community ricing committees whose members carefully observed water levels and the weather for signs that the wild rice was ripening. These men and women signaled the beginning of the fall harvest.

The wild rice harvest was the most visible expression of women's autonomy in Ojibwe society. Binding rice was an important economic activity for female workers, who within their communities expressed prior claims to rice and a legal right to use wild rice beds in rivers and lakes through this practice. Ojibwe ideas about property were not invested in patriarchy, as in European legal traditions. Therefore, when early travelers and settlers observed indigenous women working, it would have involved a paradigm shift for them to appreciate that for the Ojibwe, water was a gendered space where women held property rights. Perhaps Ojibwe women's ceremonial responsibility for water derives from these related legal traditions and economic practices. Men held a ceremonial responsibility for fire. Men traveled with their wives and female relatives to set up seasonal rice camps near the water, but they later departed to take part in the complementary occupation of hunting waterfowl or fishing.

In the ecosystem of the Lake Superior and upper Mississippi River region, where winters were long and provisions could run short, wild rice sustained the Ojibwe for a significant part of the year. The wild rice harvest, which took place at lakes and rivers in early autumn, was a model of intergenerational cooperation and learning, as collectives of women of all ages harvested and processed rice, supported by their children.[44] Nodinens' narrative captures the special place in this seasonal round for girls, who learned about labor by assisting their mothers and female relatives as they went about their work. Women continued to labor with their children and in female collectives at seasonal work sites throughout the early decades of the reservation era.

Collectives of women controlled the entire social organization of the harvest, deciding on the rules and locations of campsites. Harvesting wild rice was labor-intensive and involved many stages of cooperation. Women poled boats through the water to reach the rice, allowing a seated partner holding a pair of long, carved wooden sticks to bend the stalks over with one stick while using the other to knock rice into her canoe. When the canoe was full, the ricing partners returned to shore and the camp that had been carefully set up for processing. Women dried the green rice on large sheets of birch bark or woven mats to control moisture and mildew, which could have ruinous effects. Rice that could not be immediately dried had to be kept soaked in water.

In older times, the next stage involved smoking the rice, but the fur trade introduced utensils that allowed Ojibwe women to parch rice in a large cast-iron kettle over a wood fire to release the hull and keep the kernel from sprouting. (This kettle, called *okaadakik*, was a prized item for an Ojibwe woman, who often bequeathed hers to a daughter.) Wild rice was then hulled to remove the chaff. One method was to dance on the rice with clean moccasins—often the job of young boys. Another method was the *bootaagan*, a carved wooden mortar, which allowed women to participate, since cultural ideas prohibited menstruating women from walking over the wild rice. Historical photographs show that many different family members worked the *bootaagan*, from children to elderly men, yet one Ojibwe man mentioned that even though he helped his mother with this work as a child, "the third thrashing, Mother did. She refused to leave this to any of the children."[45] The final step involved winnowing the rice to remove any remaining chaff. Women often sewed together large birch-bark trays with basswood fiber for this purpose. They stood under the full sun to vigorously toss rice into the air, allowing the breeze to carry away the last of the chaff.

Men and women possessed a vast body of knowledge regarding their native ecosystem's extensive inventory of plant and animal life based on generations of experiment and study. They understood that wild rice followed four-year cycles, that it was vulnerable to weather and water levels, and that the harvest could fall short. Agricultural production varied from year to year. The lack of insulating snow in winter, late-spring frosts, or too-dry summers with little rainfall caused wild blueberries to wither on the vine. Yet, from this yearly cycle of mobility and environmental variability, Ojibwe people derived a strong sense of resilience and security. Nodinens expressed her family's experience with a sustainable Ojibwe way of living when she said, "When I was young everything was very systematic."[46]

Ojibwe identity and political organization were also very systematic and historically were closely aligned with kinship networks. In the evolution of Ojibwe society by the time of European contact in the Great Lakes region, families, communities, and the *doodem* developed social and political mechanisms that controlled and apportioned resources. Ojibwe people often describe this tradition as one that dates from a time before Anishinaabeg, when the earth was new, and name as their original clans the crane, catfish, loon, bear, marten, and moose, though a great many more *doodem* existed by the eighteenth century. In Ojibwe cosmology the world is animated by spiritual power; birds were on the earth long before animals, and some stories suggest that the partridge, *bine*, was created first as the mother of all birds. Birds and animals possessed intelligence and understood seasons, weather, hunting, procreation, and the importance of making a home; it was fortunate that they preceded our human ancestors by a long time, because without them the original people may never have survived. Underlying the *doodem* tradition was a deeply held regard for the relationship between the human and animal worlds, as described in the Earth Diver story, one of the principal creation stories among the original peoples of North America.[47]

Ojibwe people relate that, in a time long ago when the world was covered by water, the first earth was brought to the surface by a small animal, the muskrat. It succeeded in diving into the water and bringing back a bit of dirt to a spirit woman after several animals—the beaver, marten, and loon—had tried and failed, and the muskrat itself almost perished in the effort. For that reason, speakers of the Ojibwe language respectfully refer to the muskrat as Wazhashk, or "survivor." This first earth was placed on a turtle's back, and from that earth a new world was created.

While the muskrat was tended and restored to health, the spirit woman painted the rim of the turtle's back with the small amount of soil that had been brought back to her. She breathed upon it and into it the breath of life. Immediately, the soil grew, covered the turtle's back, and formed an island. The island formed in this way was called Mishe Mackinakong, the place of the Great Turtle's back, now known as Michilimackinac. The island home grew in size. As the waters subsided, the animals brought grasses, flowers, trees, and food-bearing plants to the sky-woman. Into each she infused her life-giving breath and they lived once more. In the same way were the animals who had drowned revived. Everything was restored on that island home. At last the time came for the sky-woman to fulfill the promise of life. One cloudless morning she gave birth to twins, a boy and a girl. They were composite in nature, made up of physical substance and a soul-spirit substance. In this respect they were similar, yet at the same time they encompassed vast differences. One was a man; the other was woman. The new men and women were called "Anishnabeg," beings made out of nothing, because their substances were not rock, or fire, or water, or wind. They were "spontaneous beings."[48]

When Ojibwe people tell stories about creation, they often describe the earth, Aki, as gendered, as woman. The *doodem* was quite literally the breast from which milk and sustenance derived and was the center of one's spiritual identity.[49] An Ojibwe writer interprets the term *doodem* to mean "that from which I draw my purpose, meaning, and being."[50] Ojibwe people maintained spiritual ties with a particular *doodem* from the animal world, and an individual or family carried the identity of crane, loon, or other *doodem* from place to place as they traveled for trade or ceremony, which allowed for a dynamic, ever-evolving reciprocity from multiple Ojibwe communities as they moved around the Great Lakes region.[51]

When the French and other Europeans first encountered large gatherings of Anishinaabeg, they typically referred to the political organization they observed in culturally familiar terms and called them "nations." The Ojibwe relied on the indigenous concept of *doodem* to explain their relationships, which differed greatly from European political entities and concepts. In fact, the Ojibwe organized their political and social worlds through their kinship networks, and from the *doodem* they derived their sense of "nation," which allowed them access to land and resources in seasonal cycles of movement that brought them into frequent contact with other Anishinaabeg, making negotiation and diplomacy indispensable to community well-being and political alliance.

Like many other North American Indians, Ojibwe people in the Great Lakes region did not live or conduct politics within the confines of a bounded geographic space but, rather, seasonally moved within their homelands, returning every year to the best places for gathering, farming, fishing, hunting, making maple sugar, and harvesting wild rice. Patterns of seasonal travel within a familiar landscape were essential to the economy of a community, shaping sustainable practices that had a number of sound environmental, economic, and social functions. Men followed migrating birds and spawning fish and traveled to the transition zone that joined the woods and prairie to hunt the white-tailed deer. Women's mobility was governed by the ripening of seasonal foods. Some food supplies were available only at certain times of the year, while other seasonal movements helped the Ojibwe manage resources, including fish and game.

The Ojibwe lived according to a seasonal round, each year taking advantage of opportunities to hunt, fish, farm, and gather wild foods in a highly systematic way of life. The seasonal round sustained the early European travelers and missionaries in Anishinaabewaki and opened the door to new trading opportunities. It was a way of life passed down by the generations and required study, observation of the natural world, experimentation, relationships with other living beings on the earth, and knowledge-generating labor. Ojibwe stories still recall a time before history, and the importance of their first grandmother, Nokomis, whose grandson Nanabozhoo discovered a lake full of wild rice ready to fall from its stalks. Pitifully, he could only look at the rice; he had few abilities. To harvest *manoomin*, he relied on the skills and woodland tools of the only woman who survived in his world, his grandmother Nokomis.

2

MADELINE ISLAND

Ojibwe Women in Fur Trade Society

❈

THE VILLAGE AT Chequamegon on Gichigamiing, or Lake Superior, was an active crossroads in the indigenous exchange with French fur traders that began in the seventeenth century. Gichigamiing was an indigenous space where every place in the panorama was marked by the presence of native people and cultures, even as the fur trade influenced the political economy of the western Great Lakes region until declining in the 1830s. As viable as this economy was for a long period, the fur trade did not replace Ojibwe social structures or values with European ones. The most successful traders learned to speak Ojibwemowin, the Ojibwe language, and married into the indigenous families of Gichigamiing. The Anishinaabeg were a self-reliant majority, who—along with a smaller number of relatives who were Métis, or people of mixed heritage—incorporated European trade and people into their economy and community.

The southern shore of Gichigamiing, particularly the long, narrow portion the Anishinaabeg named Chequamegon following their historic migration, was a critically important economic and political landscape for several centuries. Even before the years of the fur trade, marriage alliances allowed the Ojibwe to incorporate assorted outsiders into their social network, which later enabled them to establish mutually beneficial ties with Europeans in the Great Lakes region. Ojibwe people considered kinship the center of human relationships within the *doodem*, yet their clan system was one that encouraged fluidity and the possibility of new partnerships and connections between peoples. As the fur trade encouraged greater proximity and relationships between the Ojibwe and European traders, Ojibwe women in fur trade communities formed influential and intimate associations with European traders. These men required a regular stream of skins and food, and indigenous women controlled the greater part of the harvested food supply.[1]

One of the first lessons of the fur trade for European men was that their success depended on conducting business with Ojibwe women, in addition to men. Any resistance to the idea could jeopardize their own survival. The necessities of the fur trade made permeable the borders of Ojibwe and European society, with marriages between newcomers and indigenous women becoming the foundation upon which new cultural relations were constructed in the Great Lakes.[2] Building these relationships involved negotiating completely different understandings about how to organize gender roles and community life, but ultimately the unions deeply influenced day-to-day interactions in the society around Gichigamiing's southern shore.

Stories remind us that Madeline Island, the largest of the red-cliffed islands clustered in Chequamegon Bay, was named for Madeleine Cadotte, a distinguished Ojibwe woman of the Crane clan who married a fur trader.[3] The Cadotte family provides a remarkable example of the great reach of mixed marriages across time and cultures. Madeleine Cadotte lived a very long life in the eighteenth and nineteenth centuries and was the daughter, wife, mother, and grandmother of influential men and women. In her prime, her life story as an Ojibwe woman was remade by her marriage to Michel Cadotte, a fur trader who was himself of multicultural heritage. Michel had established the fur post at La Pointe on the island. He was known to all the residents of and travelers to the southern shore of Lake Superior, and his children with Madeleine grew up in fur trade society. As a wife and mother Madeleine lived through a period of widespread social disruption when the Ojibwe negotiated a number of treaties and confronted removal. After she passed away, her granddaughters and other descendants were among the early settlers of the White Earth Reservation.

First and foremost, Madeleine Cadotte was the daughter of White Crane, the leader of the historic Ojibwe community at La Pointe. Her Crane *doodem* has been translated literally as "echo maker," a reference to the strong, resonant voice of the long-legged bird. The Crane clan was widespread in the southern part of the Gichigamiing region, and many members of the *doodem* inherited the crane's resilient call as a gift for oratory. A number of significant Ojibwe leaders were members of the Crane *doodem*, including those who signed early treaties (at Montreal in 1701, in Wisconsin at Prairie du Chien in 1825, and at Fond du Lac in 1826) with a symbolic drawing of the crane.

Madeleine Cadotte probably received her European first name when she married Michel in a Catholic ceremony at Sault Ste. Marie. The island where the couple lived and worked was renamed Madeline Island in later years but in their lifetime was called by the original Ojibwe place-name, Mooningwanekaaning, a reference to birds that lived there.[4] Her family spoke Ojibwe and would have used her Ojibwe name, which is remembered in English translation as Traveling Woman. Little is known about Madeleine's early life, before she married Michel Cadotte sometime during the last decade of the eighteenth century. He had arrived at La Pointe after working trading sites along the St. Croix and Mississippi Rivers in the fur trade business he had inherited from his father. The Cadotte family surname Madeleine adopted upon her marriage was a sign she had entered a new legal relationship.

Michel Cadotte had grown up in a culturally diverse community at Sault Ste. Marie, a site of historic villages dominated by Anishinaabeg, especially during the summer fishing season. He was the child of a French trader and an Ojibwe mother, Anastasie, of "great energy and force of character" who was known for "the influence she held over her relations," the chiefs of the Awaazisii *doodem*, from which fish clans originated.[5] Anastasie was not only powerful but very active in the family's fur trade interests. She traveled by canoe for long distances from Sault Ste. Marie, accompanied only by the *coureurs du bois* ("runners of the woods"), to establish trade relationships with other indigenous communities. Michel Cadotte followed in his father's footsteps in business and in life by making an advantageous marriage to the daughter of a significant Ojibwe leader, which made possible his success as head trader on the southern shore of Lake Superior. His personal and professional life blended two very different cultural and economic traditions.

Marriages such as those between Michel Cadotte's mother and father made strategic sense, but they did not succeed easily. European traders and settlers arrived in the Ojibwe homeland with very little firsthand knowledge of the environment or the economy of the people who lived in the region, and they had a poor grasp of indigenous ways of life. Early encounters were full of misunderstanding. But in time, both Great Lakes traders and indigenous people came to speak more than one language (Ojibwemowin became one of the important languages of the fur trade), and they were increasingly able to communicate within their dynamic social world. Ojibwe people supplied essential goods and services to traders and other newcomers to the Great Lakes, in addition to allowing them to move into and profit from the resources of their country. One early-nineteenth-century English fur trader, George Nelson, came to the Gichigamiing region at the age of fifteen and soon married a young Ojibwe woman, the first of two Ojibwe wives. In his journals Nelson remarked that his men were entirely dependent upon the Ojibwe "for our very existence, & still were so blind that we could not understand." Nelson's admittedly naïve first encounters are at odds with the popular image of the carefree and capable trader, most at home in the wilderness. His Ojibwe father-in-law "had to hunt & fish for us," while he was as helpless as a suckling.[6] Nelson was fortunate to find a tolerant father-in-law, since Ojibwe men were expected to hunt for their in-laws during the period of amity that is the first year of marriage. Most likely, Nelson's father-in-law saw opportunity in having family connections to a European trader.

The first traders in the Great Lakes region arrived without wives or families. During the early decades of the trade, indigenous people traveled by canoe to the settlements at Montreal, bringing their furs to trade with the French. The center of the fur trade eventually relocated to the indigenous communities as the French sought to gain access to the inland trade, where the richest winter beaver coats were located. In the early seventeenth century, Ojibwe people were already living at La Pointe, the main village on Madeline Island, one of the first communities settled on the shores of Gichigamiing. In the fall of 1659, the well-known French explorers and trading partners Médard Chouart des Groseilliers and Pierre Radisson came to Chequamegon Bay, where they later built a fort and benefited from the large sturgeon and pike that residents fished from the waters. They established ties and trading networks with Ojibwe and other people in the region, then traveled south to Lac Courte Oreilles before returning to Quebec with a large quantity of furs. French ventures into the region continued when, in 1669, the French missionary priest Jacques Marquette followed traders to La Pointe and began to spread Catholicism.

The fur trade was less of a masculine world when the exchange came to be located in indigenous communities, as French traders from Montreal or Detroit traveled to the interior. Anastasie's efforts show how essential it was for traders to find native partners, male or female, to accompany them to indigenous communities. Madeline Island was strategically located in Lake Superior, one of a number of waterways (including Green Bay in Wisconsin, the Wabash River in Indiana, the St. Joseph River in Michigan, and the Illinois, Kaskaskia, and Mississippi Rivers in Illinois) that were important in the fur trade with the French. After Great Britain's military victory over France in 1760, and through the American period in the Great Lakes region, Madeline Island remained a center of the fur trade between the British and American companies and the Lake Superior Ojibwe. Lake Superior was also one of the best sources of the beaver coat, and Madeline Island was one of many indigenous landscapes in the Great Lakes region where Ojibwe women worked and formed partnerships with European newcomers that benefited their families and communities.

La Pointe was an active trading community for many years before Madeleine Cadotte was born. In 1762 the main fur trade post was closed during the continuing struggle between Great Britain and France, and in 1793 Michel Cadotte opened the first permanent post after the French withdrawal from the region. After the War of 1812, the American Fur Company maintained the trading post, where Michel Cadotte had served as an agent of the British North

West Company. After more than two decades on the island, he acquired American citizenship and began to work for the American Fur Company around 1816, the year of the Indian Trade and Intercourse Act, as Congress mandated that only citizens be granted trading licenses to do business with indigenous tribes within the borders of the United States. These political changes were not of great consequence on the southern shore of Gichigamiing, which remained socially and demographically an Ojibwe and Métis community in the early nineteenth century.

The culture of trading communities expected men like Michel Cadotte to take Ojibwe wives and form a network with their indigenous relatives, who, in turn, held them to a high standard that emphasized reciprocity. Cadotte fulfilled those expectations, first by making the strategically advantageous marriage during his first years on the island and then by involving his indigenous and other relatives in the operation. Michel Cadotte had learned a great deal about the trading business at Sault Ste. Marie from both his French father and his enterprising Ojibwe mother. Madeleine and Michel Cadotte raised a large family on the island, and she eventually came to be considered a matriarch of the region.

Two of their daughters followed the family tradition by marrying traders: Charlotte and Marie Cadotte married Hudson's Bay Company employees who were also siblings, Truman and Lyman Warren. They followed their mother's pattern of giving children European names but speaking Ojibwe. The Warren brothers came to the western Great Lakes region from New England in the aftermath of the Indian Trade and Intercourse Act, and eventually, in 1823, purchased their father-in-law Michel's interest in the fur trade post at La Pointe. The following decades were years of population growth and prosperity on Madeline Island, a time when La Pointe was the Michigan, Wisconsin, and Minnesota headquarters of the

American Fur Company. Madeleine Cadotte and her French-Ojibwe daughters, Charlotte and Marie Warren, lived most of their years as wives of fur traders. Though these daughters married Protestant New Englanders and had French ancestry, they communicated exclusively in the Ojibwe language of their mother and her *doodem*.

These women expanded the Ojibwe idea of what kinds of work a woman could do. Men and women followed a gendered division of labor that served their society well, but it was not so rigid that women could not take on a unique role in their community, especially one that benefited the greater good, as being the wife of a fur trader did. Madeleine Cadotte's Ojibwe mother-in-law, Anastasie, known for the dynamic way she conducted business and influenced her important family, was obviously a leading figure in the Great Lakes fur trade. Her willingness to travel long distances accompanied primarily by French men bears out her reputation for independence. Her family connections and power allowed her to build a strong network of relationships with native communities. An Ojibwe story from the Gichigamiing region makes an important point about women in community life who, like Anastasie, assumed new roles and responsibilities. This story relates the unusual experiences of a woman who married a beaver.

A woman was once fasting when there appeared to her a human being. When taken to his home, he turned out to be a beaver. She became wife to him, and lived the life of the beaver with him. By and by she returned home and told of the attitude of the beavers toward human kind.[7]

At first, the woman did not realize she had married a beaver, and they had four children; as time went on, she had to admit that something was strange about her husband. The woman became a liaison between humans and animals, especially after her husband died and she returned to the human world. Scholars note that the story has parallels to Ojibwe women in the fur trade, who similarly crossed boundaries and served as intermediaries, sometimes through the intimacy of marriage.[8]

It was not just matriarchs like Anastasie and Madeleine who regularly dealt with Europeans. In the world of the Cadotte family on Lake Superior, Ojibwe women managed much of the food supply, which positioned them at the center of the tribe's public life in dealing with traders. Women's labor was fundamental to the success of the seasonal economy. Apart from the meats, fish, and other provisions men brought in, women produced enough food to store a huge quantity that could last their families through long winters in the Great Lakes region, frequently with a surplus that they were able to barter and sell. Once the fur trade became centered in Indian communities, women's labor was also essential to the fur trade economy. The military explorer Zebulon Pike recorded in his journals a North West Company settlement at the turn of the nineteenth century that subsisted on "great quantities" of "wild oats," or wild rice, as their primary staple food, which was purchased from Ojibwe women "at the rate of about one dollar and a half per bushel."[9]

Traders carried some provisions with them, but it was an absolute necessity for them to acquire food from indigenous people. The fur trade was a system more deeply complex than the mere exchange of European merchandise for furs supplied by indigenous men. In fact, Ojibwe men and women had an array of opportunities and ways of partaking in the fur trade.[10] As George Nelson, the English trader, confirmed of his experience in the Great Lakes region, receiving food was a central part of the trading relationship with indigenous people. Ojibwe men supplied meat and fish, yet survival also depended upon the food supply that Ojibwe women produced and controlled. Considering the variety of ways in which Ojibwe women participated in the trade, one historian has suggested, "it may be that women were more often involved in direct trade than men."[11] The supply of food that native women or their families provided was critical; as Nelson wrote in 1804, "We subsiste [*sic*] upon Indian charity."[12]

As with the Ojibwe round, the fur trade also followed a seasonal cycle. In due course this new seasonal round became familiar to Ojibwe women, who took a leading role in incorporating European trade goods into their labor and households. Traders arrived in the fall, bringing clothing, blankets, cloth, and utensils, which they used to purchase food for winter survival. The exchange no doubt included quantities of recently harvested wild rice (easily stored, transported, and extremely nutritious) and maple sugar left over from spring. Traders visited Indian families to receive furs in both winter and spring, and after trading posts were established, native people brought in furs. The seasonal cycle of trade ended in the spring. The credit system used in the region meant that spring pelts were often a form of payment for items obtained in the fall. Some gifts exchanged were ceremonial. At other times, labor was a source of exchange, because Ojibwe men and women had the skill and natural resources to make and repair canoes for traders.

Alcohol was another, often darker element of the exchange. Binge drinking was introduced by European traders, and while it may have been a social ritual or a coping mechanism during a period of cultural adaptation and tension, it sometimes had a destructive effect on family and community life. In his autobiography, *The Falcon*, John Tanner—a Euro-American who was adopted by an Ojibwe family and married an Ojibwe woman around

1800—described "seasons of drunkenness" in fur trade society. He complained that even his adoptive Ottawa mother, Netnokwa, had a taste for rum, though he clearly admired her many remarkable qualities.[13] Writer Louise Erdrich, in her introduction to a modern edition of Tanner's book, describes Netnokwa as "charismatic and hilarious," "a prophetic dreamer who occasionally drinks to excess," and the "most arresting character in the drama of Tanner's life."[14] Despite Netnokwa's alcohol use, she steered Tanner through a period of sickness and despondency when he considered taking his own life.[15]

Traders' encampments were legendary for hard drinking, and the practice was never confined to men, native people, or the working classes. Tanner mentioned an important dinner during a council with Lewis Cass, the politician seeking to establish American colonial authority over the economy and native people of the western Great Lakes region, who "asked me to drink wine with them," after which Tanner was "scarce able to walk home." Governor Cass commented on the Indian fondness "for intoxicating liquors" during a long evening of festive drinking in which he and his guests clearly overindulged. Yet life was not a blur of perpetual drunkenness; binge drinking in fur trade society was moderated by long spells of sobriety when alcohol was not at hand.[16]

Hardship, high mortality, and other losses may have contributed to alcohol abuse by Europeans and Indians during the years of the fur trade. John Tanner's narrative included an account of the time he traveled with Netnokwa, who intended to take a considerable supply of beaver and otter skins to Mackinac. When they were detained at Grand Portage, Minnesota, she asked a female relative to take the furs on to Mackinac. A French trader of the North West Company issued a "due bill" for the furs, but it was destroyed when fire engulfed their lodge. Netnokwa never received compensation for losing what amounted to months of labor, and Tanner observed that she "began to drink" after "the disappointment of her hopes of returning to Lake Huron, and other misfortunes."[17]

Tanner's frequently dramatic narrative also describes a horrific period of disease among the Ojibwe; even among those who survived, "some were permanently deaf, others injured in their intellects, and some, in the fury occasioned by the disease, dashed themselves against trees and rocks, breaking their arms or otherwise maiming themselves." Tanner also contracted the illness and said of the widespread suffering, "This disease was entirely new to the Indians."[18] Various epidemics took their toll on Ojibwe life during the early years of encounter, including smallpox and other virulent diseases. A deadly virus with no cure, smallpox was feared, especially in an age when the practice of inoculation was not widespread in the geographically isolated Great Lakes region. Ojibwe people found that smallpox spread easily when groups of people gathered together, and families hastily dispersed to avoid it once it appeared, their only defense against a terrifying and fatal disease.

One Lake Superior Ojibwe elder recalled her family's tragic encounter with smallpox during the nineteenth century. Madeline Cloud, or Naganabenazekwa, was raised by her grandfather Mike Bayeasha, who was a fur trader, and her grandmother Ogeego.[19] When she was a small child, her parents died in a smallpox epidemic that struck too swiftly to allow her family to escape intact. Cloud related her story in the 1930s to Marie Denomie, an Ojibwe writer for the WPA, who sketched out the following account:

> The first recollection of Naganabenazekwa was that of seeing her grandmother, Ogee-go, and her grandfather, Mike Ba-yea-sha, crying. She wondered what it was all about, and looking across the camp fire, she saw her mother,

Be-mo-say-kwa, lying down, covered with a blanket. She was later told that her mother had died of the Small Pox.

Whole families had been wiped out by this horrible plague, including Kay-ka-qunce, her father, who was a full-blood. The Indians feared that the disease would exterminate all of them, and in panic fled for safety. Naganabenazekwa, with her parents and grandparents, were also in flight when the scourge overtook them.[20]

Fortunately, Madeline Cloud did not contract the disease and was left with devoted grandparents to care for her. She went on to have not only a happy childhood but a long life. Cloud attributed her survival to extended kin and community, saying she deeply loved her grandparents, who each provided for her in their own way—her grandfather by hunting and her grandmother by seasonally harvesting food. She emphasized the spirit of cooperation that existed in her childhood: "It was the custom of the Indians to share with their neighbors the benefit of the hunt. They lived as one large family, sharing with each other whatever they had."[21]

The presence of Europeans and the formation of new economic relationships between indigenous people and their trading partners had already created profound social changes in places like Madeline Island and the surrounding Chequamegon area of Gichigamiing by the early nineteenth century. Many indigenous women had married European or Euro-American men, making it possible for the political economy of the fur trade to expand and for personal alliances to produce new structures of kinship in Anishinaabewaki. The most successful unions for traders were marriages to the daughters of leading Ojibwe families. Along with the partnerships represented by the Cadotte family, other marriages with prominent Ojibwe women further cemented mutually reciprocal relations.

The daughter of Chief Buffalo of La Pointe married trader Benjamin G. Armstrong during the 1840s, giving him entree into the Lake Superior Ojibwe communities.[22]

One early Sault Ste. Marie trader, John Johnston, came to Madeline Island in 1791 and tried to forge a marriage with Ozhawguscodaywaquay, or Green Prairie Woman, the daughter of Waubojeeg, or White Fisher, a hereditary leader of the Caribou *doodem* at Chequamegon.[23] White Fisher was skeptical of the union, having witnessed too many short-term alliances between traders and Ojibwe women, without the give-and-take expected by the Ojibwe community. Johnston eventually did prove his steadiness to White Fisher and married Green Prairie Woman in 1792. They raised eight children after resettling at Sault Ste. Marie. Their marriage lasted several decades as he worked as a major Lake Superior trader. Like many Ojibwe women married to traders, Green Prairie Woman continued to engage in the seasonal round and speak her indigenous language. She received the territorial governor, Lewis Cass, when he arrived in the Ojibwe community to negotiate the Treaty of Sault Ste. Marie in 1820. Cass was an arrogant diplomat who offended clan leaders upon his arrival, and it was Green Prairie Woman who stepped in to defuse an alarming confrontation between him and the Ojibwe.[24]

In 1823 Johnston and Green Prairie Woman's daughter Bamewawagezhikaquay, or Jane Johnston, married Henry Rowe Schoolcraft, the early Indian superintendent for Michigan Territory, who worked at Sault Ste. Marie. They inhabited a world that has been described as "culturally hybrid" for its movement between French, English, and Ojibwe language and culture, politics and commerce. Jane learned English and reading at home, where her British father kept a library, and traveled to England and Ireland with him as a girl. Still, her mother's cultural influence was strongly present in her life, evident when Johnston sent to Schoolcraft during the courtship birch-bark *makakoons*, small baskets of maple sugar. She is also regarded as the earliest literary writer of American Indian ancestry, with fifty poems in English and Ojibwe, in addition to Ojibwe songs and oral narratives she translated into English. While some may note the influence of Jane Johnston's father in her literary efforts, she also spoke her mother's language and referred to herself as Bamewawagezhikaquay in some of her writing.[25]

Ojibwe women were valued for their influential kinship networks, yet mixed marriages were not without difficulties. White Fisher's concerns about traders taking advantage of indigenous women had a deep basis in fact.[26] In forming relationships with traders, women and their children risked abandonment by the more itinerant workers. Not all traders were alike in their motives or circumstances; Hudson's Bay Company employees seem to have had more lasting relationships with indigenous women, whereas the greater mobility of the North West employees discouraged permanence.[27] Some fur trade pairings lasted only a single season. In particular, indigenous women living in Montreal or distant from their relatives were in a weaker position. However, when women had the benefit of kin, they were more protected from physical or other abuse or premature marriage and had more options in the case of desertion. Even when this was the case, some Ojibwe women found fur traders less than ideal partners. While many examples exist of long, successful unions between native women and European traders, George Nelson recounted his own poor treatment of two Ojibwe wives, which in the wisdom of his later years he regretted. He wrote that some Ojibwe women could not "be prevailed upon to live with traders."[28]

Historians writing about the Great Lakes fur trade of the United States and Canada have emphasized *à la façon du pays* ("in the custom of the country"), fur trade society marriages that brought together elements of European and indigenous traditions to create distinctive communities.[29] Such marriages took place even though initially the Hudson's Bay Company officially forbade them. Intermarriage within fur trade families gave rise to a supportive structure for family and social relations. Women supplied moccasins, snowshoes, fresh and dried foods, and small game and helped make and repair canoes. They also had knowledge of the landscape and language, making them skilled interpreters and diplomatic agents. Daughters, such as Charlotte and Marie Cadotte, who grew up in fur trade society and had been instructed by their Ojibwe mother, no doubt cultivated many useful skills.

The question of how the subordinate place of women in Western society influenced the position of indigenous women, especially the many who also had European fathers and relatives and resided in fur trade society, is an important issue in coming to terms with Ojibwe women's history. Ojibwe society considered gender roles to be mutually supportive, valued the collective labor practices of women, and respected their legal rights, especially in regard to water. The European societies they encountered were dominated by much more patriarchal views of gender, which prompts the question of whether the daughters of European or Euro-American traders and indigenous women were more vulnerable to a system that prioritized the trader's needs. It has often been assumed that nineteenth-century values and codes of conduct in Europe and the United States and Canada "diminished the standing of native women," though such assumptions spring from encounters with Euro-American sources, rather than the indigenous societies in which women also interacted.[30] Analysis of the status of women and attitudes toward the offspring of fur trade marriages, especially daughters, from trade company records, church records, or traders' journals sheds light on the racism, discrimination, abandonment, and other inequities these women faced within Euro-American society. Females of mixed ancestry do not fare well in many historical sources. Yet these same documents say next to nothing about how Ojibwe women were regarded by indigenous people, who conferred not only spiritual power but a significant legal and economic role on women.

On the other hand, it has also been proposed that if indigenous women found lesser standing in European marriages, they also led less burdensome lives within the fur trade community. And as time passed and unions continued to grow through generations, the shock of the new wore off, especially as fur trade marriages continued to produce children of blended ancestry. Indeed, fur trade employees increasingly married women of mixed Indian and European heritage, or women from Europe, after the merger of the Hudson's Bay and North West companies that took place in the 1820s.[31] Prior to that time, most officers and employees had married indigenous women.

Along with women, indigenous and mixed-heritage children also played a role in developing economic and kinship ties between Europeans and the Ojibwe. Emphasis upon the creation of "new peoples" and the role of women as cultural brokers in the fur trade has led to significant new interpretations of community life in the Great Lakes region, but the *doodem* also continued to define kinship and identity for people of Ojibwe ancestry. Ojibwe ideas of family, community, and identity founded upon the clan system required a pattern of relationships quite different from European traditions. It is likely that many Ojibwe children whose mothers married non-Ojibwe men from outside their community maintained intimate bonds with their indigenous kin and permanently connected these alliances between peoples.

Though it might seem obvious to conclude that American Indian women's power and status always declined in the face of European colonization, even within indigenous groups, the nature of women's continuing labor power during the fur trade years suggests a strong counterargument.[32] Their participation in the seasonal round, their firmly held rights to maple sugar groves, and the systematic labor organization used by female collectives to control the wild rice harvest assured them a constant measure of power and respect. Their efforts and products were highly valued by indigenous and some nonindigenous people at the time. European historical sources are often derogatory toward indigenous women, providing countless examples of ways in which European observers found Indian cultures and peoples inadequate, yet these views were not representative of how Ojibwe people viewed themselves or their social reality. Ojibwe men and women each had distinct roles in the fur trade based on long-standing egalitarian gender relations, and the intrusion of European cultural modes did not drastically transform these roles.

The cultural fertilization of fur trade marriages was especially apparent when it came to questions of religion. Marriages between European or Euro-American men and indigenous women almost always required Christian conversion of wives. Madeleine and Michel Cadotte were married in a Catholic ceremony, rather than *à la façon du pays.* Yet this conversion did not always have an entirely hegemonic quality; Catholicism may have offered indigenous women autonomy and independence from indigenous men.[33] Did Ojibwe women such as Traveling Woman, later Madeleine Cadotte, convert to Catholicism to break away from the authority of her important father, White Crane? If it is true that some indigenous women wishing to be freed from patriarchal decisions about whom to marry chose husbands who were French fur traders and joined the Catholic Church, it seems a poor escape from patriarchy. Even the earliest Ojibwe women who married fur traders worked to maintain the relationships that took place on the middle ground and "remain consonant with indigenous behavioral standards," because their children, extended family, and community depended on the ability of traders to procure goods and services and affirm alliances with indigenous people of the Great Lakes region.[34]

The 1830s was a time of economic decline in the fur trade, and the middle ground described by historian Richard White as a distinctive era in the Great Lakes region that connected the Atlantic and indigenous worlds had been over for many years. Demand for pelts quickly fell once silk hats replaced fur, and beaver grew scarce in aquatic environments where they had once multiplied. Ojibwe hunters turned to the trade in deerskin and muskrats to continue to make a living, and traders increasingly compensated indigenous people in alcohol. Soon Ojibwe grew indebted to traders, and traders began to look toward the U.S. government to settle Indian debts through the sale of Indian land.

This time saw intense treaty negotiation with tribes as the Indian Removal Act of 1830 dominated federal policymaking during the presidency of Andrew Jackson. With further U.S. and Canadian immigration reaching into the western Great Lakes region, it was also a time when the non-Indian population increased and treaties commenced with the Ojibwe. In a related effort, policymakers in the United States began assigning names to groupings of Ojibwe for governmental convenience during diplomacy and negotiation. The Ojibwe who lived along Gichigamiing and in the interior of Wisconsin (which became a territory in 1836) conceived of themselves as independent people organized in autonomous bands at locations the French had named L'Anse, Ontonagon, Lac Vieux Desert, La Pointe, Lac du Flambeau, Lac Courte Oreilles,

St. Croix, Fond du Lac, Grand Portage, and Bois Forte; hereafter the federal government lumped them together under the name Lake Superior Ojibwe. Similarly, Ojibwe who resided between Lake Superior and the Mississippi River were classified as the Chippewa of the Mississippi, and that designation included Ojibwe who lived at Sandy Lake, Mille Lacs, the Rum River, Gull Lake, and a number of other places in the region. Pillager became a broad designation for Ojibwe who lived near Leech Lake and north of the Mississippi River. These classifications did not reflect Ojibwe ideas about political organization; they were merely categories created by the federal bureaucracy.

Even as the United States grew in power, diplomacy with indigenous social formations was maintained through the treaty process, which recognized the self-government and inherent sovereignty of the Ojibwe. Treaties sometimes created political animosity among the Ojibwe, especially when U.S. diplomatic processes failed to take into account how the people shared land and resources, or when treaties were signed without broader consultation among clan leaders across communities. Ojibwe leaders who negotiated and signed treaties often reserved rights over land and resources for their people, even as they allowed those lands to be settled by non-Indians. Treaties were accompanied by both Euro-American and Ojibwe prayers and rituals, and the Ojibwe respected the agreements. Treaties signed into law during the nineteenth century remain legally binding documents today, forming the foundation of political relations between indigenous Americans and the U.S. government.

In Michigan Territory in 1820, after taking part in earlier treaties to establish diplomatic ties, the Ojibwe negotiated an early and very small cession of land to the U.S. government with the Treaty of Sault Ste. Marie. It involved a land cession of only sixteen square miles along the St. Marys River on the Upper Peninsula, though the Ojibwe were concerned about maintaining their access to critical fishing grounds in the region. Territorial Governor Lewis Cass was determined to build a fort in the area to support a growing American interest and desire for Anishinaabewaki—Ojibwe territory.

Indigenous women in fur trade society and their families of mixed ancestry were seldom the focus of treaty negotiation, with some exceptions. Representatives of the Lake Superior Ojibwe communities negotiated a number of treaties at mid-century, including Prairie du Chien in 1825 and Fond du Lac in 1826; the latter included annuities, money for the establishment of a school at Sault Ste. Marie, and 640 acres to be set aside for indigenous wives and children of traders.[35] Prominent traders among the Ojibwe were responsible for the addendum in the Treaty of Fond du Lac, which left out many families of mixed descent among the people called the Lake Superior Ojibwe.[36]

The early Lake Superior Ojibwe treaties, negotiated between 1837 and 1854, set the stage for an extension of American power and settler colonialism that later resulted in the creation of reservations, even as indigenous people remained demographically the majority of the population. One earlier negotiation, the 1836 Treaty of Washington, involved a large land cession in northern Michigan by the Ojibwe and the Ottawa. Debt to traders was increasingly a problem in the 1830s, and traders attended the negotiations in Washington to look after their interests. The treaty ceded significant lands in northern Michigan but also created a number of small reservations. When the treaty went to the U.S. Senate for ratification, the Senate—with Indian removal on its mind—amended it to reduce the size of the payment and to establish that the reservations be guaranteed for just a five-year term. Ojibwe and Ottawa leaders met with U.S. government representatives, including Henry Rowe

Schoolcraft, at Mackinac to discuss the amendment. Anishinaabeg leaders refused to agree to it until it was made explicitly clear that they would retain rights to use the land. When five years elapsed following the Treaty of Washington, the Ojibwe and the Ottawa did not remove west but continued life in their Michigan homelands.[37]

American interest in the pine forests of Anishinaabewaki, a northern region of what was later the territories of Wisconsin and Minnesota, motivated the 1837 Treaty of St. Peters, though it was not a removal treaty. Many dozen illegally squatting lumbermen were already cutting down trees in Anishinaabewaki by the time it was signed, and sawmills opened even before it was ratified. The declining fur trade and the Ojibwe debt to traders, many of whom resided in their communities and were relatives, were reasons for them to have an interest in negotiation. The Ojibwe negotiators assembled at Fort Snelling, above the confluence of the Minnesota and Mississippi Rivers—a place called Bdote by their Dakota neighbors and sometimes adversaries—made clear that their people had many leaders, and the negotiators could not make decisions for other autonomous Ojibwe clans. The civil chief Flat Mouth of Leech Lake described the function of the *doodem*, conceptions of collective and individual clan identity, and the role of political consensus among the Ojibwe in a speech where he made clear: "I am not the chief of the whole nation, but only of my people or tribe."[38] The negotiators complained about their growing unhappiness with traders, who freely used their resources while exchanging goods at excessive prices. Leaders like Flat Mouth understood what stakes were involved: that their people would not be able to make a living unless they continued to have access to the resources of the land and water after opening the area to settlers and lumbermen. In 1837, the Ojibwe ceded the land but retained the "privilege of hunting, fishing, and gathering the wild rice, upon the lands, the rivers and the lakes included in the territory ceded."[39]

The early Lake Superior Ojibwe treaties provide evidence of an increasing distance between the Ojibwe and their non-indigenous relatives who lived in trading communities. In 1837, fur traders looked after their collective interests and were always present at treaty negotiations to discuss the issue of Ojibwe debt to them. In fact, Lyman Warren, husband of Marie Cadotte, boasted of his success "in getting a claim of $53,000 inserted in the articles of the treaty [of 1837]."[40] For their part, the Ojibwe often advocated for including payments to traders' wives and children of mixed descent. Article 3 of the treaty explicitly stated that a "sum of one hundred thousand dollars shall be paid by the United States, to the half-breeds of the Chippewa nation" for those with ties to the ceded country, and hundreds of people came forward to receive payment in the aftermath.[41] In 1839, after claims were heard, the so-called half-breed payments of $258.40 per individual were made at La Pointe, many of them to women and children and a fair number to the direct descendants of Madeleine and Michel Cadotte. The documents related to the "half-breed" payment testimony reveal more than simple genealogical information about those who received payments; they also identify a significant change in fur trade society. Before 1834, many fur trade company employees seem to have moved every year from post to post, but after that they appear to have "established themselves in their wives' communities."[42]

Treaty negotiations between the Ojibwe and the United States launched a new chapter in the history of Madeline Island. During the 1830s treaty period, the island became first a subagency and then, fifteen years later, the La Pointe Agency, the official station of the Bureau of Indian Affairs on Lake Superior. The Treaty of La Pointe again brought together Ojibwe *doodem* from Gichigamiing and the interior lands for negotiation on Madeline Island in 1842. Ojibwe arrived by canoe, eventually numbering several thousand people. Bagone-giizhig, or Hole in the Day, the elder of Gull Lake, took part in a grand entry into the large council of Ojibwe and American representatives, accompanied by drums, rattles, and Ojibwe songs. U.S. negotiators reassured the Ojibwe leaders that the federal government was interested in purchasing mineral rights on their lands, especially to the massive copper deposits of Michigan's Keweenaw Peninsula, and that removal from the ceded land was not an immediate concern. Ojibwe leaders who signed the 1842 treaty, including Buffalo and White Crow, all had the same understanding of the treaty: that removal would not be considered until the very distant future, perhaps in fifty or even a hundred years. The federal government did not have a removal plan in place, and if peaceful relations continued between American immigrants and the Ojibwe, removal might never occur. Just as they had in 1837, U.S. negotiators confirmed Ojibwe reserved rights over the land. Both treaties are somewhat uncommon in the history of U.S.– Indian relations for their emphasis on natural resources in the ceded territory. American lumbermen and miners did immigrate to Anishinaabewaki in greater numbers after the treaties.[43]

La Pointe became the location for post-treaty annuity payments, and many Ojibwe traveled considerable distances to receive the payments owed them by the United States. Remarkably, the village at Madeline Island with a population of about six hundred people continued to prosper as the fur trade faded in importance. During the 1840s, William W. Warren, grandson of Madeleine and Michel Cadotte, was employed as an interpreter at the busy agency. Annuity goods—which included blankets, knives, guns and bullets, cloth and sewing supplies, and foods like flour and pork—were shipped to Madeline Island, and each fall the agent and interpreter issued them. Annuities were an important source of goods and income to the Ojibwe, increasingly necessary for survival. Still, problems were ubiquitous in the system. In areas of fledgling American authority, such as the western Great Lakes region, paper currency was nearly worthless, and the silver coins the Ojibwe received from annuity payments were the only substantive monetary source in the local economy. But those coins often flowed directly into traders' hands. As for the annuity goods from the government, Ojibwe complained that they were too often of inferior quality.[44]

Yet the payment of annuities also occasioned celebrations that reaffirmed elements of Ojibwe cultural identity. Julia Warren Spears, granddaughter of Madeleine and Michel Cadotte and sister of William W. Warren, recalled one annuity season, in the late summer of 1847 when she was a girl on Madeline Island, especially the exhilarating cultural events associated with the arrival of the Ojibwe clans. Spears described the traditions of reciprocity and exchange the Ojibwe practiced in the form of dance, which anthropologists in later years inaccurately designated as the Begging Dance. The Ojibwe took part in public performances on Madeline Island, transforming gatherings that might have been merely bureaucratic transfers of money and goods into a rich occasion for the celebration of human relationships. Large parties of purposefully loud and vibrantly painted dancers gave new form to annuities as a ritual exchange of gifts. Their performances were not considered begging to the Ojibwe but, instead, displays of generosity in which friendship and diplomacy were enacted among extended families, clan relatives, and visitors.

The Chippewa were arriving every day from all parts of Wisconsin Territory, and the island was very crowded when they all arrived. Their agent was James P. Hays; he was a good man. My brother, William W. Warren, was the interpreter. They were both well liked by the Indians. That year the Indians received $10 a head, and each family got a very large bundle of goods. They had rations issued out to them during payment. The day before they would start for their homes they had a custom of going to all the stores and houses and dancing for about one hour, expecting food to be given them. They went around in different parties of about 25 or 30. A party came to our house at the old fort. We were prepared for them. The day before we had cooked a lot of "Legolet bread," a lot of boiled salt pork, and cookies to give them. They came dancing and hooting. They were naked, with breechcloths, their bodies painted with black, red, yellow, vermilion, with all kinds of stripes and figures. They were a fierce-looking crowd. They were all good dancers. After they were through they sat down on the grass and smoked. We gave them their food, and they were well pleased. They thanked us and shook hands with us all as they left.[45]

The early treaty era in the Great Lakes coincided with a time of religious conversion among the Ojibwe, though the area had long been home to entreaties by European missionaries. Madeline Island itself was not only a critically important economic and political landscape; it was also a place shaped by the spiritual practices of generations of Ojibwe people. The long design of the Midewiwin Lodge, Midewigaan, is said to suggest the shape of the waters of Gichigamiing. Since the arrival of Jesuit missionaries in the seventeenth century, the island had been a significant outpost in the history of Catholicism in the Great Lakes. Father Claude Allouez established a small mission, La Pointe de Saint Esprit, in the 1660s, though he is largely remembered for angering the local indigenous people, who burned down his chapel, forcing his departure in 1668. The priest Jacques Marquette, who produced the first European map of the Mississippi Valley after a canoe trip to Anishinaabewaki, also experienced difficulty at Chequamegon and left for Sault Ste. Marie in 1671. Catholic French Canadian employees of the fur trade companies spread their faith among their indigenous relatives, as did Protestants who worked in the fur trade and married into indigenous families, yet there was no formal missionary enterprise at Madeline Island for many decades. Some company employees desired a European, Christian education for their children, though fewer girls than boys were sent away to Canada or England for schooling.

For a time in the 1820s, Madeline Island experienced a growth in population, when La Pointe became the regional headquarters of the American Fur Company. This was just a few years after Truman and Lyman Warren, who married the Cadotte daughters, had purchased Michel Cadotte's interest in the fur trade post. In the 1830s, the Warrens, who were Protestant, persuaded the American Board of Commissioners for Foreign Missions, in Boston, to open a school and Protestant mission on Madeline Island. Their children attended this school along with indigenous children, their cousins also of mixed ancestry, and other offspring of French, English, and Scottish fur trade employees. The Great Lakes Métis identity, which has been widely discussed among scholars, was a significant part of fur trade culture and society. Still, the Ojibwe language was the "universal speech of the territory" even as late as the 1830s, when children in the school had books in Ojibwemowin.[46] Missionary Sherman Hall operated the Madeline Island school, and he complained about his Catholic rivals and the Ojibwe and their children, who continued to participate in a seasonal migration and economy that left them little time for a Christian education. The Ojibwe resisted his missionary efforts; many who maintained their spiritual beliefs and ideas of the afterlife insisted to Hall, after hearing his message, that they "go to a different place when they die."[47]

As the Ojibwe refused to take part in conversion, politics and competition between Catholic and Protestant missionaries grew acrimonious in the Great Lakes. In 1835, missionary priest Frederic Baraga (remembered for his linguistic skill and for completing an early dictionary in the Ojibwe language) came to Madeline Island to work with the Ojibwe, and a permanent Catholic church was constructed in 1841. Sherman Hall resented the intrusion of his Catholic counterpart and worked to prevent Baraga from receiving government funding to open a Catholic school on the island.

It is not clear how religious issues concerned or divided the Cadotte-Warren family, who negotiated a range of Christian religious and Ojibwe spiritual influences within their community. The Cadotte complex of relatives at La Pointe included both Catholics and Protestants. Madeleine and Michel were Catholic and raised their daughter Marie Cadotte Warren in the faith and to speak Ojibwe. Yet Marie married a Protestant New Englander, and their children, who were bilingual, attended Protestant schools. Even so, Catholicism remained in parts of the Cadotte line, and Frederic Baraga's first baptism on the island was Madeleine and Michel Cadotte's nine-month-old granddaughter, Elizabeth.[48] The Protestant school on Madeline Island emphasized English, though missionaries conversed with students in Ojibwemowin and used a New Testament translated into the indigenous language. Church services were also bilingual. Baraga, who embraced the indigenous languages of the Great Lakes region, favored instruction in Ojibwemowin.

Just as Madeline Island served as an important center of the Great Lakes fur trade, it became a hub for Protestant missionary activity in Wisconsin and Minnesota Territories.[49] Protestant funds allowed for a log church to be built on the island; it was completed in 1839, and at some point in its history the interior walls were completely papered with square sheets of birch bark, the versatile organic material Ojibwe women adapted to so many uses. Around the time of all the Protestant missionary activity, the American Fur Company relocated to the western part of the island, away from where the Cadotte family had worked a post for three decades. The company had some success at diversifying its operation to include commercial fishing, yet it went bankrupt in the early 1840s and ended its business in 1847, the year trader Lyman Warren died on the island. Also that year, a smallpox epidemic killed eighteen people on Madeline Island, and many Ojibwe were subsequently inoculated against the disease when they came to collect their annuity payments.[50]

The United States steadily pushed its authority onto Anishinaabewaki and other indigenous territories in the middle of the nineteenth century, but well before that time Christianizing the Ojibwe and other Indians had been a piloting project. Politicians, reformers, and many citizens believed that Indians would never be a part of American life if they would not change their spiritual beliefs in ways that conformed to Christianity. Even as the government voiced ideas of Indian assimilation, citizenship, and inclusion, it advanced policies to undermine these goals through separation, removal, and exclusion. It is no coincidence that the Protestant mission grounds on Madeline Island served as the site of another major negotiation between the Ojibwe and the U.S. government in 1854, though this time the discourse was fixed on concentrating the Ojibwe on reservations.

That year, thousands of Ojibwe gathered at La Pointe; many came to negotiate permanent homelands, seeking to affirm their rights and resolve the ambiguities of earlier treaties regarding Ojibwe who lived on lands ceded in 1837 and 1842. In fact, the government's official designation of some Ojibwe as Lake Superior and others as Mississippi was also problematic, but the 1854 Treaty of La Pointe attempted to identify groups as one or the other and to assign those groups to reservations within their homelands. Much was at stake, as the government's plan allowed Mississippi Ojibwe to collect annuities from the sale of Lake Superior Ojibwe lands, leading to new tensions between people and communities. The 1854 treaty also affirmed Ojibwe hunting, fishing, and gathering rights, as the leaders once again maintained that they could not make a living on the resources of the reservations alone.

The Treaty of La Pointe divided the historic Ojibwe community at Madeline Island, whose ancestors had followed the *miigis* shell and migrated together to Gichigamiing and Chequamegon Bay so many generations ago. The treaty gave four sections of land (later enlarged) to Chief Buffalo's community across the water, on the Bayfield Peninsula at Red Cliff. The remainder of the La Pointe Band retained a large reservation of seven townships, which included a Protestant settlement at Odanah. The Bad River Ojibwe retained a section of shoreline and exclusive fishing rights on the northern end of Madeline Island.[51] Historians have emphasized how Catholicism and Protestantism drove a wedge between the Ojibwe after the treaty, but in reality the Ojibwe people continued to regard one another as relatives, and some never fully abandoned the Midewewin and other indigenous spiritual practices. Ojibwe who lived on reservations at some distance from Lake Superior, including Lac du Flambeau and Lac Courte Oreilles, still returned to the area for ceremonial and economic reasons.

William Whipple Warren, the historian and grandson of Madeleine and Michel Cadotte, died young, in 1853, at age twenty-eight from tuberculosis, but he knew his grandmother well throughout his short life and benefited from her stories as he wrote the remarkable manuscript that would be published some thirty years after his death as the *History of the Ojibway People.*[52] Even as "Madame Cadotte" approached the age of ninety, Warren wrote that the "old woman's memory is still good" and included her oral histories of fur traders and the Ojibwe in his narratives. Her multicultural grandchildren, the Warren siblings and cousins, the descendants of the fur trade at Gichigamiing, were the first generation to be completely bilingual. Warren was well-known for his work as a government interpreter, as well as a significant scholar and an oral historian with the Ojibwe people. Aside from its place in her grandson's history, Madeleine Cadotte's name would live on in that of Madeline Island as well as in the name of a great-granddaughter, William Whipple Warren's daughter Madeline Warren, who moved to the newly created White Earth Reservation in Minnesota during a new era of social disruption for Ojibwe communities.

History books have not forgotten the name of Michel Cadotte, either. His Ojibwe mother, Anastasie, his wife, Madeleine, and his daughters, Charlotte and Marie, are often mentioned in passing, but it was Cadotte's female relatives who connected through marriage and clan the network of goods and people upon which the Great Lakes fur trade depended. Some descendants of this multiethnic fur trade family remained at Lake Superior, though others spread out to join relatives, marry, or find employment in northern Minnesota and Wisconsin on newly created reservations. Ojibwe and other indigenous women assumed new roles during the fur trade, which contributed to the prosperity of their communities. Outsiders entered the Ojibwe web of kinship relations through marriage and the birth of children, giving rise to new bonds of family. For a people who understood kinship through the *doodem*, even new people who married into the family were bound in reciprocal relations of protection, goodwill, and generosity.[53]

The question remains open as to how the women and children of the fur trade, with roots in indigenous and nonindigenous families, thought of their own identity. There is evidence from the writings left by Madeleine Cadotte's grandchildren, especially William W. Warren and his sister Julia Warren Spears, that suggests they saw themselves as a people apart from the Ojibwe, even as they worked and lived out their lives in close proximity to Ojibwe communities. Educated in Eastern schools, raised as Protestant and bilingual, the Warrens and their cousins may have constructed their own identity and community differently than did their mothers and grandparents, or even than their own children who settled at White Earth and other reservations. For certain, their grandparents and parents actively participated in the shaping of an ethnically and culturally diverse world in the Great Lakes region. Their own children and grandchildren would experience a difficult age when America's racial hierarchy became further entrenched through the establishment of the reservation system, and people of mixed race coped with limited opportunities within a harsh regime if they continued to live among their Ojibwe relatives. The extension of American colonial authority into the western Great Lakes region that began in the 1830s was more than a political struggle over Ojibwe homelands and the creation of reservations in Gichigamiing and the upper Mississippi: it struck as a century-long landslide that unbalanced carefully constructed places for women's autonomy in community life.

3

RESERVATIONS

Holding Our World Together

❦

MINDIMOOYENH, the Ojibwe term for a female elder, best embodies how Ojibwe society has traditionally perceived women's power. In the Ojibwe language, it literally refers to *"one who holds things together"* and is a category of distinction that honors the pivotal role occupied by fully mature women in the social order.[1] Older women were given unconditional respect. They were recognized for possessing a hard-earned wisdom that derived from firsthand experience with life's passages: puberty, giving birth, raising children, contending with sickness and disease, and enduring the infirmities or death of parents and other loved ones. Women's power was an expression of how the Anishinaabeg understood the world they inhabited. In contrast to Europeans, for them, humans were just one small part of a world intensely alive with spiritual power, making it important to respect, accommodate, and maintain kinship with the other living beings that share the earth. Older women, who often had a ceremonial tie and expertise with plants and medicines, had a more finely attuned connection to the earth's *manidoo*, or spiritual power. Through their labor and control over certain resources, women continuously renewed relationships to their relatives in the human and spirit world. In day-to-day life, *"one who holds things together"* was a reference to the economic competence and organizational skill that Ojibwe women, especially grandmothers and those in their maturity, exercised within their families and communities. Far more than merely designating an "old lady," *mindimooyenh*—an idea born of women's autonomy—evokes the status, strength, wisdom, and authority of the older female in Ojibwe society.

The wisdom of elders and the security derived from women's roles were called on to hold things together as the complex and widespread social disruptions of the reservation era tested the political and communal resources of the Ojibwe people. During the 1830s, politicians and power brokers in the United States focused their attention on indigenous communities of Gichigamiing and the upper Mississippi and began a more concerted effort to remove, consolidate, "civilize," and negotiate land sales with the Ojibwe. As long as the Ojibwe retained control over their lands and resources, the border between British Canada and the United States had little meaning for them, and local indigenous politics and activities persisted. Each negotiation forged a new problem, and for decades after the middle of the nineteenth century the growing nation-states of Canada and the United States steadily pursued the acquisition of Indian lands. Each treaty forced the Ojibwe to make impossibly difficult decisions, which they understood would influence future generations, yet they remained steadfast in pursuit of their way of life.

For Ojibwe women and their communities, the reservation era produced profound change, which involved adapting the seasonal round to include a variety of informal economic strategies within a world of diminishing resources and increasing poverty. Women adjusted even as they lost access to environments crucial to their live-lihood. Federal authorities and missionary organizations launched countless intrusions into family privacy and community life under the banner of assimilation, the process through which indigenous men and women were to be culturally remade in the image of Euro-Americans. Once again, land was the issue, though the discourse of assimilation advocated Indian citizenship and incorporation into the body politic of the United States.

Later in the nineteenth century, when local and state authorities embarked on strategies to violate the legality of reserved treaty rights, the Ojibwe began to carry a new burden, which grew with every denial of the right to use their essential resources—the wild rice, fish, game, maple sugar, and gathered fruits and medicinal plants that ensured their health and survival. Gender roles and carefully crafted work practices of men and women were also vul-nerable to the pressures of assimilation and government programs, as customary Euro-American notions of masculine and feminine labor were obsessively promoted among all the indigenous peoples in the United States. Cultural and political sovereignty was obstructed on all fronts. The Ojibwe learned early that politicians and agents of the United States who crossed their homeland posed a real threat to their existence.

One of the early reservation era assaults on the Ojibwe is referred to as the Sandy Lake Tragedy, an event chronicled by Julia Warren Spears and a few others at the time but remembered today by hardly anyone other than the Ojibwe.[2] At Sandy Lake, on the Mississippi River in central Minnesota, an episode of ethnic cleansing took place in the mid-nineteenth century when the United States attempted to remove Ojibwe from their homelands in the newly established state of Wisconsin to Minnesota Territory. One hundred seventy Ojibwe died at Sandy Lake, and 230 more succumbed on the long walk home to Wisconsin and Michigan. The devastation resulted in a population loss of about 12 percent among Wisconsin Ojibwe at mid-century. Those estimated four hundred deaths do not take into account the Minnesota Mississippi bands of Ojibwe who perished as they traveled home from Sandy Lake, stories of which were written down by missionaries at Leech Lake. More Ojibwe people died as a direct result of the atrocity at Sandy Lake than the estimated two hundred Cheyenne massacred at Sand Creek or the three hundred Lakota slaughtered at Wounded Knee.

The governor of the newly organized Minnesota Territory, Alexander Ramsey, had a particularly intimate role in the removal plan and the incidents that unfolded at Sandy Lake during the early winter of 1850. In that year, Ramsey chose Sandy Lake, the home of some Ojibwe communities, as the site of a new Indian agency to replace the one at Madeline Island. A son of political patronage, Ramsey favored the development of a Northern Indian Territory, one that fell within his jurisdiction, with all the associated government funding opportunities and Indian annuities. He collaborated with John S. Watrous, a La Pointe trader of questionable reputation who was appointed special agent for removal in 1850, on a furtive plan to remove the Ojibwe from their Wisconsin homelands. Their deception was essentially to set a trap for removal by calling Ojibwe families to Sandy Lake for an annuity payment, then to detain them in the Minnesota Territory as they waited for the annuities to arrive. If the payments arrived late in the season, it would mean that the Wisconsin Ojibwe would be unable to travel home when waterways froze.

Ramsey was deeply involved, both politically and financially, in the development of the region. The treaties negotiated in Anishinaabewaki in 1837 and 1842 involved land cessions in the western Wisconsin and Minnesota Territories, in addition to exchanges of goods, annuities, the payment of debts to traders, and a compromise that established the preservation of significant rights to continue Ojibwe economic lifeways over the land. In the fall of 1849, Ramsey and the Minnesota Territorial Legislative Assembly collaborated to invalidate portions of the 1837 and 1842 treaties with the Lake Superior Ojibwe and called for their removal based on false and unsubstantiated claims of "depredations" against white settlers. In fact, these claims were made at a time when the Ojibwe argued that violence and theft toward them by lumbermen, settlers, and other new immigrants went unpunished and even uninvestigated by Minnesota authorities. Governor Ramsey followed up the actions of the assembly with a visit to Washington, intended to convince President Zachary Taylor of the necessity for Ojibwe removal to Minnesota. U.S. Secretary of the Interior Thomas Ewing and Commissioner of Indian Affairs Orlando Brown approved the plan. At a moment when traders and local economies were very reliant on Ojibwe annuities and income, the location of where the payments were made was very important. Henry Rice, a trader and Minnesota politician who had much to gain from moving the Ojibwe payment to Minnesota Territory, was also an advocate for the removal. He wrote to Ramsey:

> They should receive their annuities on the Mississippi River, say at or near Sandy Lake, at which place an agency for the whole tribe should be established. This would better accommodate the whole tribe and Minnesota would reap the benefit whereas now their annuities pass via Detroit and not one dollar do our inhabitants get altho' we are subject to all the annoyance given by those Indians.[3]

From the standpoint of Minnesota Territory politicians, the issues of Ojibwe removal from Wisconsin and the relocation of the site of annuity payments from La Pointe, on Madeline Island, to Minnesota were closely intertwined. On February 6, 1850, President Taylor issued an executive order that overstepped his authority by revoking the reserved rights to hunt, fish, and gather for which Ojibwe leaders had so judiciously negotiated when they ceded territory under the treaties of 1837 and 1842 and signed an agreement with the United States. The 1850 executive order also called for the removal of "all said Indians remaining on the lands ceded."[4] The Lake Superior Ojibwe uniformly opposed the Removal Order of 1850, which required thousands of people to leave their ancestral homelands and travel hundreds of miles to the Mississippi River in northern Minnesota, thereby intruding on the lands of other Ojibwe people. It was an inconceivable proposition. Past assurances to the Ojibwe that they would remain on the land for many years, perhaps 150, or until the present generation had passed away, and that annuities would be regularly paid to them, meant little to federal and territorial authorities, who turned against the promises made by their own government by threatening the withdrawal of annuities if the Ojibwe failed to remove.

Faced with little choice, many Wisconsin Ojibwe came to Sandy Lake for the annuity payment in the autumn of 1850, traveling several hundred miles by land and water and arriving in late October. Julia Warren Spears described the hard journey that many Ojibwe from Wisconsin undertook. She went to Sandy Lake with her brother, William W. Warren, who was already suffering the effects of tuberculosis, in the event that he became sick during the trip. He survived but would die just three years after Sandy Lake.

The account by Julia Warren Spears is significant for its detail regarding how the Ojibwe sustained themselves during a long journey, by carrying with them wild rice, flour, and pork and by hunting along the way. It also describes the food shortages and dire circumstances the travelers soon faced at the government's temporary annuity camp at Sandy Lake. Spears recalled traveling up the Chippewa River to Lac Courte Oreilles, where her party picked up a group of Lac du Flambeau Ojibwe, and the "next day we started on our journey through the woods." She continued:

The Indians packing their canoes, they all had packs of some kind on their backs. We had to walk nearly all day. We came to a lake and camped for the night. Our tent was put up, with branches of spruce and cedar spread on the ground in the inside, which made it quite comfortable. In front outside of the tent, a small fire, where I cooked our evening meal. The Indians built several large camp fires, fixed places to hang their kettles over the fire, to cook their evening meal, which was large kettles of wild rice and flour soup, water thickened with flour seasoned with pork. It was always their evening meal, as it took a short time to cook. On each side of the fire they stick small poles to hang long rush mats for a covering where they slept. A number of them were hunting through the woods as we traveled along. They killed all kinds of game such as deer, geese, ducks, and other game. Some of them would cook by the fire nearly all night, game they had killed during the day, and cooking legalet, bread made with salt, water, and flour, kneaded quite hard in round flat loaves fastened on stick and placed before the fire.[5]

Spears, William W. Warren, and the growing party of travelers crossed many rivers and lakes before reaching the St. Croix River, where they waited several days for the Pokegama and St. Croix Ojibwe to arrive. Once joined together, the parties moved on toward Lake Superior and canoed down a treacherous stretch of the Iron

River, which, despite its many obstacles and rapids, the expert Ojibwe traversed with ease. By the time they reached the present site of Duluth, there were seven hundred Ojibwe from Wisconsin camped. The Ojibwe travelers went on to Fond du Lac and crossed "a three day portage" to Sandy Lake before their three-week journey ended. It was an exhausting trip, Spears recalled, but when they crossed Sandy Lake to arrive at the agency, "all the Mississippi Bands of Chippewas and Leach [sic] Lake Indians with their families were all there, waiting for the payment."[6]

Thousands of Ojibwe arrived at Sandy Lake in time for the annuity payment to be held, on October 25, 1850. The unusually large convergence of Ojibwe in north-central Minnesota coincided with a year of food shortages for the bands near Sandy Lake on the Mississippi River. That fall the local wild rice crop had failed because of flooding on the Mississippi, and fishing had also been poor. With food in short supply for those gathered, the situation worsened when Indian agent John S. Watrous failed to arrive at Sandy Lake on the date when he was supposed to deliver the annuities. The provisions of food that had been promised were also delayed. Weeks passed without the payment, and soon winter set in. The Ojibwe waited and waited. For sustenance they were forced to rely on the food supplied by the government, mostly flour and salt pork, but what arrived turned out to be moldy, spoiled, and unfit for consumption, leading to widespread hunger and sickness.

During a six-week interval in the early winter of 1850, approximately 170 of the estimated 4,000 Ojibwe people assembled at Sandy Lake died. Watrous finally arrived and completed the annuity payments on December 3, 1850. After weeks of meager and contaminated food, illness, and death, the Wisconsin Ojibwe left

Sandy Lake; but now, already weakened, they faced grueling winter weather. On the trip back home to Wisconsin and upper Michigan through deep snow and bitter cold, an estimated 230 more Ojibwe lost their lives. Travelers abandoned their canoes when the waterways froze, and survivors walked home, sometimes crossing hundreds of miles.

Approximately 1,500 Ojibwe from northern Minnesota—Leech Lake and other communities—had also attended the annuity payment, and some of their number also perished after leaving Sandy Lake. Their bleak return journey was similar to the harrowing events in Wisconsin, when Ojibwe who had already experienced deprivation at Sandy Lake contracted dysentery and other diseases, with many never making it to their destination. It is not clear how many deaths from northern Minnesota were counted, or if any at all were included, in the 400 estimated by the Lake Superior headmen shortly after the event.

A missionary's wife in northern Minnesota described how the Ojibwe at Leech Lake remembered Sandy Lake as "the burying-place of their friends" and related appalling stories of hunger, sickness, and suffering. She learned of a brother and sister from Cass Lake who were returning home in the deep winter when the brother took sick shortly after leaving Sandy Lake and subsequently died halfway to Leech Lake. The sister refused to leave her brother's body in the snow and waited two days for another group to come by and assist her with his burial. Stories of the Mississippi Ojibwe from northern Minnesota suggest that women and families traveled to the annuity payment debacle at Sandy Lake, not just men. The missionary's wife told of her close neighbors, another Ojibwe family who had been at Sandy Lake and intended to return to Leech Lake. The husband and wife reached home but carried with them their two young deceased children. She related their somber story:

This family consisting of a man and his wife, two children, and his wife's brother, started from Sandy Lake in health, with food enough for their journey, if they had not been detained on their way. About half-way from Sandy Lake to Leech Lake, the wife's brother was taken sick, and detained them several days, when he died; they buried him and came on. Three days' march from Leech Lake, the two children were taken sick, the oldest a boy of twelve years old (who, by the way, was the best boy we have known in the country, a member of our school, one we had hoped to educate), the other a girl two years old. At this time their food was all gone. The father was obliged to carry his sick son, and the mother the daughter, until the last night before they reached Leech Lake, when the boy died. The next morning they set off again, the father carrying the corpse of his son, and the mother a sick child. About noon the girl died, but they came on until they reached Leech Lake, bringing the dead bodies of their children on their backs.[7]

Government reports downplayed the atrocities at Sandy Lake—Governor Ramsey characterized the Ojibwe people's claims as "highly exaggerated"—or blamed the high number of deaths simply on disease.[8] Yet Ojibwe leaders who were present at Sandy Lake continued to speak out regarding the cruelty and disregard for humanity their people had experienced. Bagone-giizhig, the Mississippi leader from Gull Lake known as Hole in the Day, gave a speech in St. Paul describing the spoiled food and moldy flour the Ojibwe were given, which caused the initial sickness, and the long days and nights at Sandy Lake during which five or more people expired on a daily basis. Eventually he concluded that "the more treaties we make the more miserable we become."[9]

After the events of Sandy Lake, Ojibwe people were increasingly convinced that federal and territorial authorities desired their removal or, worse, their extermination. Eshkibagikoozhe, or Flat Mouth, the Mississippi leader from Leech Lake, had also been at Sandy Lake and was unequivocal that the events were not the result of accident. He placed blame directly in the hands of Alexander Ramsey. "I lay it all to him," said Flat Mouth, in a mocking reference to "our Great Father the Governor," who was responsible for making his people suffer "by sickness, by death, by hunger and cold." Flat Mouth reproached Ramsey for making the Ojibwe attend the payment during the essential hunting and fishing season and said, "If we had remained at home we should have been far better off than we are now with our scanty annuity." While at Sandy Lake, the Ojibwe had been promised food and provisions, yet ultimately they "had to depend upon the charity of our fellow Indians." Flat Mouth relayed to Ramsey a firm message of culpability: "Tell him I blame him for the children we have lost, for the sickness we have suffered and for the hunger we have endured."[10]

Ojibwe people have never forgotten Sandy Lake. A woman from the Sandy Lake region of Minnesota, Mrs. George Curtis, daughter of an Ojibwe leader from the area, shared her family's memory during the 1920s. Even though her words were recorded decades later, they were eerily similar to the observations, shortly after the events, of William W. Warren, who related the sentiments of Wisconsin Ojibwe who felt the United States planned "to poison them off, to hurry their removal from Wisconsin."[11] Such feelings cannot help but seem validated in the face of historical evidence, which overwhelmingly demonstrates that Sandy Lake, regardless of the role played by bureaucratic neglect, was not an accident. In the aftermath, Ojibwe leaders expressed clearly their conviction that the government plan was removal, regardless of the cost to human life.[12]

Deaths from starvation, sickness, exposure, and other suffering that transpired during the winter of 1850 had catastrophic consequences for Ojibwe women, families, and community life, though perhaps a greater number of men than women or children died. Some distant Ojibwe communities that refused to come to Sandy Lake so late in the season were spared, including the L'Anse, Ontonagon, Pelican Lake, and Lac Vieux Desert. A few Wisconsin Ojibwe communities prudently sent only their men, even though the government intentionally asked that families come for the annuities, believing that removal would succeed only if families were present at Sandy Lake. Mississippi Ojibwe communities and others closer to Sandy Lake appear to have traveled with their families. Historians believe that one-third of the Lake Superior Ojibwe's most able-bodied male hunters and fishermen, and female workers in the traditional economy, died as a direct result of the inhumanity that unraveled at Sandy Lake. Starvation and disease disproportionately killed people in the prime of life, and the consequences would reverberate in the Ojibwe population for years to come.[13]

In the aftermath, twenty-eight Lake Superior head chiefs signed a document that described the agent's deception and testified to their trauma and that estimated the number of total dead among their people at four hundred. They explained:

When we left for home, we saw the ground covered with the graves of our children and relatives. One hundred and seventy had died during the payment. Many too, of our young men and women fell by the way and when we had reached home and made a careful estimate of our loss of life, we found that two hundred and thirty more had died on our way home. [14]

The devastating events of Sandy Lake lingered in the historical memory of the Ojibwe people and their leaders in the years after 1850, coloring all future negotiation with the U.S. government. Ramsey, Watrous, and other government officials had proven not simply untrustworthy but capable of a callous disregard toward human life. Ojibwe leaders, forced to deal with Watrous the following year and still challenged with removal, stated, "At the next council, we told him [Watrous] we wanted our last year's payment, that our children were cold and we had not money to buy them clothing."[15] In 1851 the L'Anse Ojibwe made formal charges against Watrous that included "broken promises and daily deception," unethical conduct stemming from "a practice of seducing and cohabiting with our women," and attempting to create his own chiefs and leaders through bribery, which has "broken up the civil polity of our tribe."[16] Frustrated over removal and with receiving little response to their letters and petitions, an Ojibwe delegation traveled to Washington in the spring of 1852, led by the distinguished leader of the Lake Superior headmen, Bizhiki, Chief Buffalo of La Pointe.

Though Bizhiki was more than ninety years of age and the oldest of the Lake Superior leaders, he was eager to travel to Washington, "just as soon as my canoe will float on the Lake in the Spring."[17] By canoe, steamboat, and rail, the delegation made the two-month journey, the first leg of which Bizhiki and the Ojibwe spent gathering signatures of support from miners and other non-Indian residents along southern Lake Superior.

It is not certain whether Bizhiki ever had his audience with President Millard Fillmore while in Washington, but in some ways the first stage of his journey was the more interesting. During his travels, he successfully gathered the support of many settlers and non-Indian citizens who were convinced that it was in their own best interest for the Ojibwe to remain in their homelands of Wisconsin and Minnesota. These settlers had arrived after the busiest years of the fur trade, and in many ways they interacted with indigenous residents like the early generation of traders: they cultivated relationships of exchange. The development of mining along the south shore of Lake Superior in the mid-nineteenth century had encouraged Ojibwe communities in the region to increase their farming labor. They then sold surplus vegetables to the growing population of miners. The food Ojibwe women gathered—especially their surplus of wild rice, berries, and maple sugar—was another mainstay for the settlers, who also relied on the women for clothing and moccasins. Ojibwe women and their communities had proven to be excellent neighbors and essential contributors to the growth and development of the regional economy, and new settlers were not eager for them to go west.

In a written statement presented to President Fillmore and other Indian Affairs officials, Bizhiki chose a simple yet powerful woodland metaphor to argue for the Ojibwe right to sovereignty and their homelands. First, he commented on the traumatic Sandy Lake events, the suffering and unnecessary Ojibwe deaths that resulted, and the promises that had been made to his people during negotiations over the Treaty of La Pointe in 1842. The elderly and exceptionally well-spoken Bizhiki delivered his message through imagery that he believed the president would easily grasp. He challenged Washington by offering a new paradigm for Indian-American interaction, one in which harmonious relations might exist, and he urged sensible behavior in the American settlement of his people's homelands. He suggested this example: when white men enter a new country and decide on a place to settle, they might choose to cut away the brush and bad trees so that the ground can be leveled. At the same time, he reasoned, good, healthy trees would never be cut down. Bizhiki urged the president to consider the Ojibwe the same as "the good trees," which should be allowed "to stand and live."[18]

Shortly after Chief Buffalo's delegation visited Washington, a change in administration and Indian Affairs shifted federal policy away from removal to concentration on reservations. Beginning in 1854, the hard work of petitioning for reservations on their homelands in Michigan, Wisconsin, and Minnesota began to yield results for the Ojibwe. They were supported by a large contingent of non-Indian citizens in Wisconsin and Michigan who joined the lobby to end the removal. Great Lakes–area newspapers were also highly critical of Washington and supportive of the need for permanent reservations.[19] A refocused Indian policy in Washington, led by Commissioner of Indian Affairs George Manypenny, resulted in new treaties, the establishment of reservation lands, and a shift toward education for "civilization," rather than the concept of total removal that had dominated since the Jacksonian years.[20] The new Treaty of La Pointe, in 1854, officially organized Ojibwe of the Lake Superior or the Mississippi Band, though some communities were left out of the negotiation. The treaty also created Ojibwe reservations. As a consequence, Ojibwe bands on Lake Superior and in the interior of Wisconsin, including some on the Upper Peninsula of Michigan, were designated as Lake Superior Ojibwe and received reservations at L'Anse, Ontonagon, Lac Vieux Desert, La Pointe, Lac Courte Oreilles, Lac du Flambeau, Grand Portage, Fond du Lac, and Bois Forte.

As part of the "civilization" policy favored by Manypenny, Ojibwe land tenure practices wherein women held usufruct rights to maple sugar groves and wild rice waterways were disregarded in favor of western notions of private property, and tribes were forced to cede crucial landscapes. The Detroit Treaty of 1855 failed to protect the rights of the Ojibwe to interests in their important Sault rapids fishery and also introduced a private property allotment scheme for Ojibwe and Ottawa descendants of participants in an earlier treaty of 1836. Leaders of six Sault bands, including Canadian Garden River Ojibwe, took part in the Detroit treaties and negotiated for small, permanent places of residence in their homelands. Ojibwe in Michigan had owned all of the Upper Peninsula prior to the Treaty of 1820 but lost millions of acres in 1836. The Detroit Treaty of 1855 was not the agreement they had hoped for, yet Ojibwe persistence in its aftermath allowed for their continuing presence in northern Michigan.

At the beginning of the nineteenth century, Ojibwe people firmly controlled the upper Mississippi, but during the territorial years, from 1849 to 1858, immigration and westward expansion turned Minnesota into one of the fastest-growing regions in the country. In 1850, American Indians were still the majority population in Minnesota Territory, but during the next decade they were overrun in numbers by a settler society, with a new state and constituents increasingly bent on exploiting the forests of the northern Great Lakes region.[21] The 1855 Treaty of Washington, led by Commissioner Manypenny in Washington and Henry Rice in Minnesota, negotiated with several delegations of Mississippi, Pillager, and Lake Winnibigoshish leaders, led by Bagone-giizhig from Gull Lake and Flat Mouth from Leech Lake. The treaty acquired an enormous land cession from Ojibwe in northern Minnesota for the United States and entailed substantial payments, as well as annuities and goods, for the Ojibwe for a period of thirty years, in addition to the establishment of reservations. Ojibwe treaty rights over ceded lands had already been affirmed in 1837, 1842, and 1854, prior to the 1855 negotiation. Red Lake leaders negotiated treaties of land cession in 1863 and 1864 but never relocated from their homeland.

The goal of further concentration on northern reservations fueled U.S. government Indian policy in Minnesota during the 1860s, despite Ojibwe objections. The Treaty of 1867 created a large reservation in northern Minnesota, White Earth, intended as a new homeland for all the Minnesota Ojibwe, though one leader protested that his people would "die first in our old homes" rather than agree to removal.[22] In the atmosphere of Ulysses S. Grant's "Peace Policy," various religious organizations grew in influence on the new reservations, and at White Earth missionaries linked masculine agricultural practice with Christianity. White Earth Ojibwe increased their farming while maintaining as long as possible communal practices associated with the traditional seasonal economy.[23]

The White Earth Reservation encompassed farmlands, wild rice lakes, and forests and was a place where policymakers envisioned that relocated Ojibwe would come together to live as settled farmers, embracing Christianity and education. White Earth became the center of a statewide effort to consolidate and privatize land through allotment among the Ojibwe who lived within the borders of Minnesota. A number of Madeleine Cadotte's grandchildren, including Julia Warren Spears and Mary Warren English, arrived at White Earth during the removals of 1868–70, shortly after the creation of the reservation. Like their family, a number of other people in the community were of mixed Ojibwe and Euro-American ancestry, including the Beaulieu, Morrison, and Fairbanks families. Truman Warren, another Warren sibling, was hired as overseer by the United States for the first Ojibwe removals from Crow Wing and Gull Lake to White Earth. By 1876, hundreds of Ojibwe from northern Minnesota and Wisconsin had come to White Earth, in addition to many Pembina Ojibwe from the Turtle Mountains of North Dakota.

The 1887 Dawes General Allotment Act in the United States spearheaded a nationwide effort to assimilate Indians into the mainstream of American society by promoting Christianity, education in off-reservation boarding schools for children, and the privatization of reservation land. In Minnesota, land allotment was given additional impetus by the 1889 Nelson Act. This legislation turned political attention to the twelve Ojibwe reservations in the north, as consolidation and allotment at White Earth were viewed as the statewide solution to the "Indian Problem." Policymakers, missionaries, and other reformers promoted the idea that private ownership of land, agricultural labor, and Christian values would lead Indians to progress, citizenship, and salvation. At a time in the United States when some national leaders favored extinguishing all native claims to land—and in Minnesota where, in the aftermath of the War of 1862, the Dakota had been executed, imprisoned, or exiled from their homeland—many non-Indians elevated allotment and assimilation as nothing short of humanitarian policies.

Few reservations escaped allotment. One notable exception was that of the Red Lake community, in far northern Minnesota. Medweganoonind, at more than eighty years of age the elder spokesman among seven hereditary chiefs who represented the *doodem* at Red Lake, expressed his view of the flawed and potentially damaging land allotment policy in 1889. "I will never consent to the allotment plan," he said. "I wish to lay out a reservation here, where we can remain with our bands forever." His word held in the face of government pressure, furthering Red Lake's lasting reputation as an autonomous community, even among the Ojibwe.[24] The reservation's sovereignty came at the expense of a portion of its country: nearly three million acres of land was lost at Red Lake in 1889. But thousands of acres of land and water from their homeland were organized into a large reservation, where a communal system of land tenure continued, making it one of only a handful of U.S. reservations to avoid allotment. In 1918, the band adopted a constitutional form of tribal government that assembled a tribal council with a significant continuing leadership role for Red Lake's seven hereditary chiefs, following the older clan lines of the *doodemag*.

Most reservations would not be so fortunate. The Ojibwe experienced relentless attacks on their land and sovereignty as the reinvigorated assimilation campaign gathered strength in the late nineteenth century. While close to two thousand Ojibwe lived at White Earth at the turn of the century, others on northern Minnesota reservations resisted removal efforts, and many took allotments on their homelands, an option stipulated in the 1889 Nelson Act. In addition to Red Lake, the Mille Lacs Ojibwe people of central Minnesota were notably opposed to removal, despite the fact that their treaty rights to hunt, fish, and gather over ceded lands were increasingly being denied them and local law enforcement chose violence and harassment of the band rather than providing their legal protection. Washington resorted to an old tactic with Mille Lacs, the withholding of their annuities, but the Ojibwe maintained their right to stay in their homeland under the terms of the Treaty of 1863. Ojibwe resistance and the people's intense economic and spiritual bonds with landscapes of home meant that the White Earth consolidation plan never lived up to the expectations of Minnesota politicians and that Ojibwe community life persisted at Bois Forte, Fond du Lac, Grand Portage, Leech Lake, Mille Lacs, and Red Lake.

For tribes across the United States, the results of allotment policies and withdrawal of the protective trust relationship were economically and culturally devastating, as millions of acres passed out of Indian ownership. The Ojibwe could not avoid the environmental destruction and dispossession unleashed in northern Minnesota, Wisconsin, and Michigan in the early twentieth century. Land fraud was rampant, corruption in Indian Affairs continued unchecked, and the hollow interests of environmentally unsustainable timber companies dominated the political landscape of the northern Great Lakes region. Rather than serving as an example of Indian progress and enlightened government policy, White Earth became a national model of human suffering and environmental exploitation. By 1920 gigantic red and white pine in the once verdant tribal forest were cut-over and most of the reservation land was owned by non-Indians, taken from its indigenous owners through force or deception. Josephine Robinson described her mother's experience with the corruption that accompanied dispossession at White Earth as unscrupulous speculators singled out elderly Ojibwe for exploitation.

> I remember it was 1906. The land sharks around here got land any way they could. My mother told me how she put down her thumbprint on a piece of paper. She couldn't write. She couldn't speak English. She was a full blood. She wasn't supposed to be able to sell her land, according to the law. People didn't know what they were putting their thumbprints down for. Some thought they were renting their land.[25]

Kate Frost, a Grand Portage Ojibwe elder, had her valuable allotment of land along the scenic north shore of Lake Superior stolen. A medicine woman who spoke Ojibwe, Frost lived in

Chippewa City, near Grand Marais, Minnesota, with her grandson James Wipson (born in 1918), whom she raised for his first ten years with few resources other than what she gained from the land. Mrs. Frost suffered from arthritis, and on many days her grandson stayed home from school to help her during bouts of illness. He recalled the contentment of life with his grandmother, as well as the difficulties they faced together.

> Grand Marais was very prejudiced against the Indians. When my grandmother would take me to Grand Marais we'd walk a mile. She wanted to just get a few necessities in the grocery store. Them people wouldn't talk to us. They wouldn't pay no attention. The only one that paid attention to her was the one who was trying to get our land. Say, "Hi Katie. You need groceries?"[26]

Frost was defrauded of her land on the north shore. The friendly storekeeper who gave her flour, sugar, and salt pork was quietly paying her taxes in exchange for her "X" on a piece of paper, and the elderly woman unwittingly signed away her property, effective upon her death. The land shark, recalled her grandson, "confiscated all our land in Chippewa City," which sat on a "beautiful bay," while defrauding other Ojibwe as well.[27]

Yet even as the government forced new community organization and lifestyle changes on the Ojibwe, Frost and other women like her continued to hold things together. The deeply ingrained traditions of women's lives served as a rock that stood proudly against the winds of change and helped to sustain family and community life in the face of racial hatred, exploitation, and a desolate reservation economy of the post-allotment Great Lakes region. Women's seasonal ricing in early fall, maple sugar harvesting in spring, and berry picking in summer had even more significance to households once state game laws inhibited Ojibwe access to hunting and fishing. The Ojibwe faced arrest and relentless harassment by game wardens by the turn of the century, despite prior agreements made in good faith as the Ojibwe ceded millions of acres to the federal government. In 1897, two elderly male hunters, one seventy-two and the other eighty-eight and blind, were arrested for possessing venison in violation of state game laws and were incarcerated for four months in Iron County, Wisconsin.[28] State-sanctioned interventions onto tribal homelands and resources intensified in the post-allotment years, though men predominantly faced unjust arrest, harassment, fines, and jail terms for trespassing and violations of fish and game laws. In the case of the Iron County imprisonments, the elderly wife of one of the hunters was not jailed, yet finding her way home alone to the Lac du Flambeau Reservation with the added stress of her husband's incarceration was a cruel hardship. Ojibwe who simply hunted and gathered to make a living, exercising their legal treaty rights, had to live in fear.

In 1894, Chief Giishkitawag, or Cut-ear, who was known in English as Joe White, was murdered by a local law officer in Washburn County, Wisconsin, after he was arrested by a game warden for hunting deer out of season on Ojibwe ceded lands. The Ojibwe in northern Wisconsin had negotiated three treaties during the course of the nineteenth century that guaranteed and reserved their rights to hunt, fish, and gather over the homelands they had ceded. Nonetheless, White was arrested and the game warden struck him on the head. As he began to flee, an officer who accompanied the warden shot him from thirty yards away, and he died that day. In the spring of 1895 an all-white jury in Washburn County found the game warden and the law officer innocent of the murder of Joe White. State game laws upheld the authority, lifestyles, and desires of white, middle-class sportsmen and tourists, not those of Ojibwe families who relied on a seasonal round.[29]

Lake Superior and the Mississippi River region was a shifting environmental landscape in the early twentieth century, a fact reflected in the contrasting memories of place from one generation of Ojibwe people to the next. Maude Kegg recalled her girlhood experiences with the Ojibwe seasonal economy as it was practiced near Portage Lake, in central Minnesota, where she was born on the Mille Lacs Reservation around 1904. Kegg's grandmother Margaret Pine taught her to fish, make maple sugar, and harvest wild rice and wild fruits. Pine and other women and children sold blueberries to wholesalers, participating in the broader cash economy as an antidote to poverty. Cutover forests in Michigan, Wisconsin, and Minnesota were vulnerable to intense fires, yet remarkably these artificial conditions of regeneration gave rise to abundant crops of blueberries. Kegg and her grandmother sold their blueberries in Brainerd, a nearby non-Indian town, and fish to a wholesaler in Vineland. The northern landscape of Maude Kegg's girlhood was not the same as her grandmother's, deforested and reshaped as it was by the exertions of timber companies. Pine could recall a time when "there were so many pines that it was dark" near shimmering Lake Mille Lacs, though Kegg herself remembered the abundance of blueberries and a large logging camp that employed a number of Ojibwe laborers.[30]

Northern Wisconsin and upper Michigan were also locations for seasonal berry picking, which grew into a significant remunerative occupation in the wake of timbering, as pine forests gave way to fires that swept through and allowed for the growth of blueberries "so large and thick that it was impossible to avoid stepping on them," according to one berry picker.[31] At an active campsite on Keweenaw Point, Michigan, Ojibwe women and their families worked "burnt over" lands that now held lush berry fields. They would sell the berries "in a house-to-house canvas," providing food to Michigan's booming copper industry, then head back to pick more that would be used "for home consumption during the winter." One picker remembered:

> Next morning we started out for the blueberry fields, which were about a mile or so from the camping grounds. And berries: this is one time I beheld blueberries growing on stems four to six inches long, in clusters like grapes.
>
> Three of us, my mother, a younger sister, and myself, picked over a hundred quarts in a few hours that day. I remember that I picked a pack-box full and also a large pail full myself. The capacity of a pack-box at that time was from thirty to forty quarts; and a pail, the standard measure used in the sale of blueberries, contained ten quarts.[32]

Even after land loss, timbering, and forest fires, Ojibwe people sustained a way of life in the Great Lakes region that carefully balanced an economy of seasonally changing work sites and complementary labor for men and women. As important as wild rice was to their cycle of seasonal occupations, perfectly described by Nodinens in the early twentieth century as "very systematic," the Ojibwe never relied on this resource alone and always kept in mind the possibility of coming hardship or misfortune.[33] Female collectives organized the labor of harvesting wild rice and maple sugar, and smaller working units of women and children turned blueberry gathering into a viable source of income.

By the 1920s, Ojibwe workers in the Great Lakes had added another type of seasonal work to their annual cycle: participating in the tourist economy. Ojibwe labor was at the center of a new economy in a developing recreation landscape. Small businesses attracted indigenous laborers from reservations, who earned income near their homes and communities. Ojibwe workers in northern Wisconsin found summer employment at vacation spots like Cardinal's Resort, the Ojibwa Lodge, and Hill's Resort near the Lac du Flambeau Reservation, a community that developed an early appreciation for the rewards of tourism. Labor was gendered: women and teenagers cooked, cleaned, and did laundry, while men worked as hunting and fishing guides. Women workers also supported tourism in northern Wisconsin and Minnesota by supplying fresh berries and food for summer vacationers, in addition to manufacturing and selling crafts and handiwork large and small, from miniature beadwork trinkets to elaborate birch-bark and porcupine-quill baskets. Husband and wife entrepreneurs Benedict and Margaret Gauthier were the proprietors of the Gauthier resort on Long Lake, Lac du Flambeau's successful "modern summer hotel and cottages."[34] Sisters Bessie Stone Fisher and Sarah Stone Gilham rented out their two-story home on Fence Lake to summer visitors from Milwaukee.[35] Twenty-year-old Margaret Snow worked seasonally at the Ojibwa Lodge but in winter found time for making beadwork and moccasins before heading to the sugar bush in the spring.[36]

Married couples living on the Lac du Flambeau Reservation in the 1920s actively participated in the growing tourist economy but maintained a division of labor within a seasonal cycle not unlike that of the previous generation. Men still crafted canoes and snow-shoes in addition to hunting, trapping, and fishing, while women continued to pick and can berries, make maple sugar and syrup, and gather and process wild rice. Lizzie Young, a Lac du Flambeau Ojibwe, had a husband who worked as a summer guide while she "made moccasins, bead work, sugar, syrup, pick[ed] and can[ned] wild berries."[37] This combination of indigenous seasonal activities and wages from tourist work allowed families to purchase pianos, sewing machines, or "graphaphones." In a few instances, Ojibwe men gathered wild rice as part of their livelihood, though this probably indicated that they traveled with women to the work site and helped their family set up wild rice camp during the season.[38] Making maple syrup and sugar was also women's work, but some Ojibwe men, such as Bob Pine of Lac du Flambeau, assisted their wives.[39] During the 1920s, most married couples had children who attended boarding schools or local public schools; this may have reduced the number of available hands in the sugar bush, making men more likely to participate. The labor of harvesting maple sugar may have been more compatible with a local economy increasingly geared toward tourism, since more Lac du Flambeau women went to the early spring sugar bush than gathered wild rice in late summer.[40]

Whenever it was in the best interest of their families, women workers supplemented their normal collective patterns of labor by engaging in a variety of practices more typical of men. Widowed and divorced women who worked in reservation communities during the 1920s faced a particular set of challenges as kin networks destabilized under pressure from high rates of disease and death.[41] To earn a living, many women without partners hunted and fished, in addition to raising children and grandchildren. Helen Skye, a boarding school student at Lac du Flambeau, was supported by her grandmother through a variety of sources; even at age sixty-six, Skye's grandmother was an active hunter and trapper. Similarly, the widowed Margaret Brown gathered wild rice and also worked "like a man," according to a non-Indian observer, by hunting, trapping, and fishing, in addition to being the sole caretaker of a mentally disabled son. Mrs. Catfish, a great-grandmother, tanned hides at seventy-eight. Mattice Scott, a successful midwife with four grown children, practiced the seasonal round, in addition to crafting woven bags and reed mats and tanning hides. Perhaps to ease her burden or as a testimony to her zest for life, Scott became a new bride at age sixty-four, marrying John Batiste, her Potawatomi groom.

That women on the Lac du Flambeau Reservation hunted and fished when men were unavailable suggests that tradition did not prevail over practical concerns in the gendered division of labor. In the Ojibwe WPA narratives from the 1930s, writer Florina Denomie compiled the story of a woman from Keweenaw Bay, on Lake Superior, whom she described as "An Indian Huntress." With her grandmother's approval the huntress tracked and killed her first animal, a porcupine. Elder female relatives celebrated the event, and her grandmother's response was pride: "My girl, we will have a feast." Later, the girl tracked and killed a deer, after an uncle taught her to shoot and carry a gun. As an adult, she still wore a blouse at dances made of the tanned hide from her first deer.

> One day I went out deer hunting. I was not far from home, having been gone only about an hour, when I saw tiny hole tracks in the snow. Examining them closely, I came to the conclusion that they must be deer tracks, and I became excited and began to shiver. (In the hunter's vocabulary this is called "buck-fever.") I thought, "this will never do," and I continued in my quest for deer. I became very tired, hardly being able to lift my feet out of the snow. Finally, I tracked the deer through a small swamp. The tracks were getting fresher and my feet were getting heavier; but I managed to step over a windfall, and just as I got one foot over, up came something with a white flash in front of me, and another and another—three in all. I raised my gun and fired about a foot

of the first flash, and it went up in the air and down. (It might be well to explain that the flashes were the whites of deer tails.) I took aim at the next one, but missed. I concluded that they were all gone, and that I had missed in both shots. I thought I would go and see what I did in the first shot anyway. Imagine my surprise to find that I had succeeded in bringing down a small spiked horn buck. There it lay, with such a pleading look in its eyes, that I turned away in sorrow and tears, and while the little deer had won my complete sympathy, it was necessary for me to complete the kill.[42]

Ojibwe women re-formed their families, communities, and work habits and some of their social practices to cope with dispossession and the loss of resources on the reservation. Sometimes this involved embracing cultural changes, new identities, and different worldviews. Catholic and Episcopal missionaries continued to proselytize in northern Michigan, Wisconsin, and Minnesota, and the reservation era produced the first generation of Ojibwe clergy. Enmegahbowh, or John Johnson, an Ojibwe Episcopalian clergyman, traveled with Ojibwe to White Earth, settled on the reservation, and was the first American Indian minister of the Episcopal Church. The Benedictine order of the Catholic Church operated a boarding school for girls at White Earth and a mission and school on the Red Lake Reservation. Catholic and Episcopal missionaries worked throughout reservations in the Great Lakes, along with other Christian organizations, which relied on the skills of a bilingual clergy. In Wisconsin in 1913, Lac Courte Oreilles Ojibwe Philip Gordon became the first native person in North America to be ordained a Catholic priest. Five years later, he returned to Lac Courte Oreilles to lead the St. Francis Indian Mission. The Methodist Church was an important part of life in northern Michigan, and the Ojibwe minister Peter Marksman established the Naomikong Mission and school on Lake Superior. Part of the church's landholding was purchased by the United States to become the Bay Mills Indian Reservation.[43]

The Episcopal Ojibwe at White Earth "encouraged women to take a prominent role in community-rebuilding efforts" through their establishment of the Women's Meeting, which addressed issues related to changes in household economies and work, in addition to promoting Christian prayers and songs. The healing rituals the Episcopal women at White Earth adapted, though conducted with Christian prayer, markedly resembled those of the Midewiwin society.[44] Suzanna Wright Roy, or Equaymedogay, was the daughter of Waabojiig of Gull Lake and an early convert to the Episcopalian Church who became a Christian leader at White Earth. Scholar Michael McNally argues that, even though the women's societies were "clearly promoted to do the work of gendered cultural assimilation" and "Native women were implored to sew and cook rather than fish, rice, and gather wood," they nevertheless may have served an "energizing" role for Ojibwe women in the public life of a reservation community.[45]

While Ojibwe religious practices may have been disrupted by the introduction of Christianity, the ceremonies and philosophy of the Midewiwin, the leading religious and healing society for the Ojibwe, have had a remarkable longevity in the Great Lakes region. Ojibwe people who did not participate in ceremonies of a Midewiwin medicine lodge continued to find meaning in indigenous spiritual traditions through their belief in the healing power of song, dance, medicine, and herbs; the value of dreams and prayer; and a deep reverence for sacred places and the spiritual power of the natural world. The most important events to commemorate new life and death—naming ceremonies, feasts, funerals, and rituals of mourning—were all infused with an innate sense of Ojibwe spirituality, despite the permeation of Christianity on reservations.[46]

The Ojibwe have long used an expression, *mino-bimaadizi*, to sum up their philosophy of good living, and they define the concept as a desire to experience a long life free of sickness and misfortune. In the Ojibwe worldview, the natural world and cultural formations such as music and dance coexist in a symbiotic partnership that is essential to the good life. Regular prayers and feasts of thanksgiving were commonplace, and offerings always preceded the partaking of fish, game, and other foods. Generosity was a highly developed value on the spiritual road to a good ethical life and was ritualized in ceremony and diplomacy. Spiritual leaders passed down sacred stories in the Midewiwin. Its membership was organized around degrees in the society and required years of study and commitment. Many Ojibwe and Menominee people also incorporated *chi-dewe'igan*, or Big Drum ceremonies, into their spiritual practice during the reservation era; these originated in the late nineteenth century with the Dakota, who presented an early ceremonial drum to Mille Lacs Ojibwe. Big Drum later declined among the Dakota, though the Ojibwe have continued to practice the ceremony and remember the significant role of Tailfeather Woman, "chosen by the Great Spirit as the recipient of the first Drum."[47]

Traditional Ojibwe medicine persisted on the reservation as well. Nawajibigikwe, a woman with extraordinary knowledge of native plants and medicines, was regarded as one of the most skilled healers on the White Earth Reservation in the early twentieth century. She also composed songs related to the herbs and medicines with which she worked.[48] White Earth was rich in medicinal herbs and had areas that were ideal for gathering plants. In Ojibwe Country, a dynamic network of women like Nawajibigikwe specialized in plants and their healing properties. At White Earth, Red Lake, and elsewhere on reservations, many of the plants Ojibwe women gathered were used exclusively to address female health issues and wellness. Medicine women harvested plants in August, also the ricing month in the northern Great Lakes region. A plant was picked for its roots, stems, or leaves to make *mashkiki* (medicine). The Ojibwe approach to wellness linked the body to spiritual and emotional health, a worldview appreciated by very few Westerners who encountered American Indians living on reservations in the early twentieth century.

Government physicians who were aware of Ojibwe medicine women often trivialized their medical expertise while privileging Western ideas and approaches to the body, health, and disease, but women persisted in their work as healers. Ojibwe and non-Indians living on or near the Bay Mills community, in Michigan, in the early twentieth century relied on the skills of Ellen Marshall, who for most of her life worked as a midwife and healer.[49] Helen Goggleye, an herbalist, worked in Inger, on the Leech Lake Reservation. She grew up north of Leech Lake in a Canadian community, became the partner of a traditional healer, Joseph Goggleye, and gathered herbs for her husband.[50] Dedaatabiik, a Ojibwe woman who lived on the western boundary of the Red Lake Reservation, was an herbalist and medicine woman who doctored the Ojibwe community as well as the nearby Swedish farmers, some of whom married Ojibwe.[51] Traditional healers specialized in herbs and medicines, singing healing songs, and other spiritual activities.

These practices, especially the song and dance associated with healing, were frequently challenged when the Ojibwe interacted with government people and their institutions. Field matrons, teachers, and medical professionals hired by the Indian Office to work on reservations condemned the Ojibwe for using natural herbs and medicines and for frequenting native healers. Florence

Auginash, who attended elementary school at Red Lake during the 1940s, recalled a time when her father had carefully prepared a poultice of natural medicines for a small infection on her arm. She was distressed and hurt when the school nurse found the poultice, told her it was "dirty," and washed away all traces of her father's handiwork.[52] Doctors were confounded by the dismal state of health in reservation communities, and blamed families for creating unsanitary living conditions and contributing to high rates of tuberculosis, other disease, and disability. Ojibwe concepts of wellness, medicinal traditions, and cultural views that organized their view of the world with plants and music coexisting in symbiotic partnership came under attack in the reservation period as critics charged that these beliefs held Indians back from assimilation and racial advance, in addition to endangering their health.

In the face of this continuous pressure to curtail indigenous medicine, a significant new healing tradition emerged among Ojibwe women. During the global disaster of Spanish influenza that killed millions of people at the end of World War One, the jingle dress tradition was born.[53] Narratives from Ojibwe communities say the tradition sprang from the experience of a young girl who grew very ill and appeared to be near death. The setting is sometimes the Mille Lacs Ojibwe community in Minnesota, other times White Fish Bay, Ontario. Both communities express a great devotion to traditional forms of Ojibwe song and dance. According to the story, the sick girl's father, fearing the worst, sought a vision to save her life and through this learned of a unique dress and dance. The father made this dress for his daughter and asked her to dance a few springlike steps in which one foot was never to leave the ground. Before long, she felt stronger and continued the dance. After her recovery, she continued to dance in the special dress and eventually formed the first Jingle Dress Dance Society.

Though Ojibwe narratives recount that a man conceived the Jingle Dress Dance after receiving a vision, women were responsible for its proliferation. The first jingle dress dancer was a young girl, yet females of all ages, from youths to elders, historically embraced the tradition. Photographic images from the United States and Canada of Ojibwe women wearing jingle dresses at community pow-wows and dances began to appear shortly after World War One. Special healing songs are associated with the jingle dress, and both songs and dresses possess a strong therapeutic value. Women who participated in the Jingle Dress Dance—dancing to ensure the health and well-being of an individual, their family, or even the broader tribal community—passed the special dresses down to daughters and cherished friends.

Jingle dress dancing holds a spiritual power for Ojibwe people because of its association with healing. In the Ojibwe world, spiritual power moves through air, and sounds hold significance. The jingle dress is special because of the rows of metal cones, *ziibaaska iganan* in the Ojibwe language, that dangle from the garment and produce a pleasantly dissonant rattle as they bounce against one another, an effect that is amplified when many women dance together. When jingle dresses first appeared, they resembled women's ceremonial dresses of the era, with rows of jingles added. Dresses from the 1920s often had a sailor collar, popular in the day. Innovation is always a part of pow-wow and dance regalia, and the jingle dress is no exception, but dresses through the decades share many common features.

The Jingle Dress Dance was dream-given to the Ojibwe at a low point in their history, when they were living on reservations and looking for ways to reorder their chaotic world. Beginning in the 1920s and proceeding through each decade thereafter, photographs show Ojibwe women of every generation, from nearly every community in the United States and Canada, wearing jingle dresses. When the dress was introduced, it was an innovation, but one consistent with Ojibwe spiritual practices and traditions of song and dance.[54] The dance coincided with a new suppression of Indian religion in the United States as the Dance Order, banning ritualistic dance on reservations, arrived from Washington in 1921.

Nonetheless, the Jingle Dress Dance movement flourished, and the dance has maintained its power for nearly a century in the Great Lakes region. The dress has enduring significance, but it was especially important in shaping how Ojibwe women helped their communities mitigate the perilous effects of American colonialism and cope with reservation life at the historical moment of its origin. In every part of community and economic life related to the well-being of families and health, Ojibwe women were especially active, and the jingle dress and rituals associated with it are part of their legacy.

Wherever they lived or resettled, Ojibwe women engaged the changing world of the reservation straight on. They adapted gender roles and expectations and adjusted labor practices to new circumstances. They worked as healers within their communities and practiced what today we call holistic medicine. Women worked as the principal harvesters of wild rice and maple syrup, and gathered fruits in their communities, bringing good health and stability to Ojibwe life in years otherwise notable for land loss, deprivation, and crisis. Bay Mills, Lac du Flambeau, White Earth, and other reservations were settlements where women's efforts to hold things together merged tradition and innovation, allowing families and future generations to maintain communities in their homelands.

4

NETT LAKE

Wild Rice and the Great Depression

❁

SPIRIT ISLAND sits in the heart of Nett Lake, on what is today the Bois Forte Indian Reservation in northern Minnesota. Known as Manidoo-minis to the Ojibwe, the island is reminiscent of a drum because of the reverberations that move through the air as one walks over an area of polished rock protruding from the water. The island holds hundreds of carvings of animals, humans, and *manidoog*. Ojibwe people leave offerings of clothing, food, and tobacco at this sacred place and give thanks for the land, the water, and the wild rice. Prayers are made to the water spirits. The rock itself helps the Ojibwe observe water levels on the rice lake. Some Ojibwe who harvest rice on Nett Lake like to tell stories about *memegwesi*, small people with hairy faces who stay mostly hidden from sight but live in many ways like Anishinaabeg and harvest the *manoomin* that grows naturally in the waters bordering the island. Sometimes only the sounds of their knocking sticks are heard on the lake. Nett Lake is geographically situated north of several major watersheds, making it somewhat isolated from pollution and cut off from alterations that have negatively affected water quality and levels since the introduction of the timber industry. The 7,400-acre lake is renowned among Ojibwe people for being among the very best places to harvest wild rice, with the largest-sized grains in Minnesota.

On the surface of Nett Lake during the 1930s, the changes that the twentieth century brought to the Ojibwe way of life were made stark. For generations of Ojibwe women, water was a gendered space where they possessed property rights, which the Ojibwe conceptualized as taking responsibility for caring for the land and water and their resources. For centuries, the wild rice camp had been a female work site. Women's long-standing practice of binding rice on the lake was about more than just fending off birds and winds; instead it was one part of a highly successful indigenous legal system that empowered women. Yet the 1930s introduced changes to Ojibwe society that by the end of the decade would transform the gendered labor practices associated with the wild rice harvest and challenge the long-defined role of women in Ojibwe life.

When Ojibwe men first entered the realm of women's collective labor, they did so as wage earners and employees of government work programs. The hard times taking place nationwide in the 1930s were deeply felt in Indian Country. "An Indian family was never without meat or fruit as is now the case," mourned one St. Croix Ojibwe man. The economic pressure pushed an entire generation of Ojibwe male workers to incorporate emergency relief and conservation employment to their expanding repertoire of labor. The St. Croix Ojibwe man found it necessary to work as a pulpwood cutter for the WPA and sent his daughter to a government boarding school during the Great Depression.[1] His solutions were part of a broader trend among Ojibwe families, who survived poverty and hardship through a combination of indigenous seasonal occupations with wage labor and government relief, including boarding school education for children, where food, clothing, and instruction were paid for by the U.S. government.

Day-to-day survival during the Depression dictated that Ojibwe families separate for long stretches of time, which presented an additional hardship for a people who attached importance to the intimacy of working and living closely with kin. Throughout the Midwest, men departed for Works Progress Administration (WPA) and Civilian Conservation Corps (CCC) work camps, and children enrolled in government boarding schools. The system of segregated schooling that the federal government established for American Indians during the assimilation era had been part of Ojibwe life since the opening of the Indian Industrial School at Carlisle in 1879. In the leanest years, when resources at home were stretched impossibly thin and Ojibwe faced widespread destitution, sending children to boarding schools became a way to ensure that they were fed and clothed. Indian boarding schools had their highest enrollments during the Great Depression. Though negative attitudes and racism toward Indians may have lingered, there is evidence of greater enlightenment among teachers, staff, and administrators in U.S. Indian boarding schools during the 1930s, when most schools had formally abandoned assimilation as a goal and the federal bureaucracy was promoting ideas of cultural pluralism. It is more plausible, then, that the population peaked as students and families initiated enrollments, in spite of a long history of disdain or ambivalence about the institutions among American Indians. Ojibwe families had firsthand knowledge of the flaws of boarding schools but nonetheless sought them out for their children as a strategy of family preservation.

A study conducted during the Depression found that nearly all residents of the White Earth Reservation relied on poverty relief or pension programs.[2] Ojibwe people continued to count on their relatives and their community, vital networks where cultural patterns of reciprocity, sharing, and generosity were deeply ingrained. An ethic that encouraged one to think for others had always sustained Ojibwe life through hard times, and it played a critical role in ameliorating the effects of the Great Depression. However, decades of land loss and violations of hunting, fishing, and gathering rights were deeply felt and left the Ojibwe with few resources to navigate the perils of the 1930s.[3] Great poverty was reported across Minnesota Ojibwe communities by researchers employed in the Federal Writers' Project.

[T]he average Chippewa today lives at a bare subsistence level, and Government funds alone assure him his necessities. With the exception of the Red Lake Reservation, his lands have been allotted, and such work as he can obtain consists of mere seasonal or odd jobs. Harvesting the wild rice and blueberry crop, picking pine cones for the forest nurseries, and fishing and lumbering are only temporary remunerative tasks. Repeated attempts to re-educate the Indian in his native crafts have met with only partial success, although the tourist trade provides a lucrative market for products of his skill even when they include only the usual birchbark baskets, bird houses, and toy canoes.[4]

The Federal Writers' Project—part of the Works Progress Administration, created during Franklin Roosevelt's administration—published the state guide to Minnesota in 1938. Wisconsin's WPA project employed a number of Indian writers, and though it is not clear whether any Ojibwe numbered among the 120 writers who participated in the statewide project in Minnesota, the guide incorporated a fair amount of information on Ojibwe communities.

It described recent environmental changes on the Bois Forte Reservation and the informal economy that operated during the berry season. Perhaps most markedly, it noted a new arrangement of labor in the wild rice harvest, with men joining women on Nett Lake.

> The heavy timber that once covered the district and attracted many settlers has been cut. During the berry season, the Indians from miles around gather in swamps near the village to pick blueberries to sell. The wild rice that grows plentifully in Nett Lake also is harvested by Indians. One man paddles a large canoe while a second threshes the rice heads into it. In camp, the rice is heated in large kettles over open fires to loosen the hulls. Stalks and foreign substances then are shaken or fanned out, and the rice goes into a wooden vat, where a boy wearing moccasins "jigs" the hulls from the grain with a peculiar tramping step. Once again the rice is fanned, then weighed. Wild rice, long a staple in the Indian diet, has become a luxury food throughout the country.[5]

Wild rice gained some popularity in American cultural habits of food and drink in the 1930s but primarily as a "luxury food," never the mainstay it was to Ojibwe diets. To the Ojibwe, though wild rice varies slightly in color and size, from small seeds to large Nett Lake grains, it is always perfect. For generations prior to the Great Depression, harvesting and processing wild rice was the vocational specialty of Ojibwe, Dakota, and Menominee women workers in the Great Lakes region.[6] Through the reservation era, the lakes remained a strongly gendered space. One September in the late nineteenth century, Joseph Gilfillan, an Episcopal missionary in Minnesota, observed an estimated six hundred Ojibwe women gathered for harvest at White Earth but no men.

Traditionally, when the rice was almost ready for harvest, in late summer, men traveled with their families to set up seasonal rice camps, then worked nearby or moved farther on to fish and hunt. Collectives of women were responsible for binding the rice stalks in their pre-harvest state, knocking the ripened grain into canoes, and processing the rice in camp.

Nearly all photographs and documents about Ojibwe wild-ricing before the publication of the WPA guide and the federal work camps of the same era represent a female harvest. Some years before, the Minnesota ethnologist Frances Densmore had noted straightforwardly that "rice was harvested by women." She began her fieldwork in 1910 among Ojibwe communities in Wisconsin and Minnesota, and her ethnographically rich collection of photographs portray women's labor at every stage of production.[7] She recognized the wild rice camp as a female work site, and she photographed women paddling canoes through lakes dense with wild rice, emptying large winnowing trays full of green rice, stirring the rice on mats of birch bark with long wooden sticks, and sitting before smoky fires to parch it. Densmore was fascinated by the way women bound stalks of rice pre-harvest, correctly identifying this as a significant practice for Ojibwe women and their communities.

The long-established ritual of binding strips of basswood fiber around the stalks was fundamental to how women took responsibility for caring for the land and water and their resources. Densmore photographed and described the practice.

> Each group of relatives had its share of the rice field as it had its share of the sugar bush, and this right was never disputed. The women established it each year by going to the rice field in the middle of the summer and tying a small portion of the rice in little sheaves. The border of each tract was defined by

stakes, but this action showed that the field was to be harvested that year. [8]

For centuries in the Great Lakes, binding rice was a way for women to protect the crop in its unique ecosystem, as well as a significant part of their indigenous legal system. The Oshkaabewisag, elected ricing committees of men and women, was also responsible for taking care of their resources and held an indispensable position in organizing the harvest.[9] Albert Jenks, an anthropologist who worked in Wisconsin and Minnesota and along the Canadian border at the turn of the twentieth century, wrote in great detail about women's labor in the wild rice economy. He observed how they incorporated and instructed their children as they went about their work, and he explained the indigenous system in which female collectives not only labored together but organized the distribution of wild rice. According to Jenks' 1899 fieldwork, "the women of more than one family frequently unite their labors and divide the product according to some prearranged agreement or social custom."[10]

A similar system operated at Mille Lacs. An Ojibwe man born in 1918, Jim Clark, remembered his great-grandmother's rice camp and the decisions she made "about who would camp there"; he also spoke of how the women in his community controlled the entire social organization of the harvest on the upper lakes of the Rum River.[11] Through their labor and community-based institutions like the Oshkaabewisag, Ojibwe women constructed an extraordinary legal framework and an orderly system of ecological guardianship to manage the wild rice economy. Increased non-Indian settlement in northern Wisconsin, Minnesota, and areas along the Canadian border led to a reduced wild rice district by the time Clark's generation was born and posed further threat to the wild rice environment.

Given how important the practice of binding rice was, historically, to Ojibwe women, it is rather shocking that it disappeared in
Minnesota and Wisconsin around the end of the Great Depression,
suggesting that the prior decade was a time of revolutionary cultural change in their lives. Not only did outside intervention by
government and commercial forces change the gender balance of
the rice harvest; it also challenged the integrity of the harvest itself.
When lumbermen in Canada and the United States built dams in
order to float logs downstream to be milled, they wreaked havoc
with water levels in streams, rivers, and lakes. Wild rice grows well
in waters with gentle currents and steady water levels, but even
heavy rains can cause crop failure, and dam construction has been
lethal.[12] The creation of the seventeen-thousand-acre Chippewa
Flowage in Wisconsin by the Northern States Power Company in
1923 inundated the Lac Courte Oreilles Reservation, destroying
villages and graves and wiping out its wild rice.[13] In a similar story,
work by the U.S. Army Corps of Engineers beginning in 1884 dev-
astated native wild rice stands at the Minnesota headwaters of the
Mississippi River, and dam construction and alterations caused wild
rice that once thrived along the river to decline.[14]

Ojibwe people have observed that wild rice seems to follow
four-year cycles that include intervals when the harvest might fall
short.[15] The way of life the Ojibwe established in the Great Lakes
region was not immune to hardship. Reservation life was, for the
most part, a life of continuous economic struggle, and wage labor
became a necessity for families. When the Great Depression struck
in the United States, American Indians were among the first to lose
jobs and wages, and this additionally burdened a convergence of
colonial circumstances that had undermined Ojibwe life since the
creation of reservations. Land loss, cultural assimilation, environmental degradation, and the denial of treaty rights had already

created squalor and misery in Ojibwe Country before the unemployment and poverty of the 1930s.

At the same time, the resilient generation who remember life in the Great Depression frequently view their hard times through a lens of optimism and credit the resourcefulness of indigenous communities for allowing them to not only survive but thrive relative to other Americans. Jim Clark's view from Mille Lacs was not uncommon.

> I think people in rural areas fared better than urban people. I remember those years when my stepfather and grandma planted more than usual. My dad still had his horses. All of us kids had to help in the gardens. Our parents said it was better to do the hoeing and weeding early in the morning because everything was still damp from dew and it was cooler. We always had meat of some kind—deer, grouse, or partridge, rabbits during the winter. We used to eat porcupine, which I love, muskrats, and fish. People in the cities couldn't get this stuff and they didn't have ground for gardening, so I guess we were fortunate to have Mother Earth to depend on.[16]

The Depression years also found the Ojibwe relying more heavily on work in the tourist industry to combat the poverty in their families and communities. Guidebooks, advertisements, and postcards from northern resorts and Minnesota's Office of Tourism suggest that the opportunity to view and interact with Indians was a significant draw for vacationers who traveled to the lakes and woodlands, though genuine contact came most frequently through mundane activity performed by maids or cooks.[17] Entire Ojibwe families performed and worked in summer pageants held at

Minnesota's Itasca State Park, a fashionable tourist destination that included the headwaters of the Mississippi River, native stands of red and white pine, sparkling lakes, and the newly constructed Douglas Lodge.[18] Ojibwe workers from the surrounding White Earth, Leech Lake, and Red Lake Reservations participated in pageants at the popular "Chippewa Village," erecting teepees and wigwams, paddling birch-bark canoes, holding pow-wows, and occasionally re-enacting battles with white performers.[19] Performers could earn extra income posing for photographs; dramatic images that placed indigenous people in the past were especially popular with tourists. In one vintage 1930 Itasca postcard, a young, handsome couple with three children poses next to their fully packed travois, the mother beautifully attired in deerskin and the father in full headdress. For many decades, an "Indian Village" was a feature of the Minnesota State Fair, peaking in popularity during the 1930s. In 1935, the WPA sponsored a state fair pow-wow in St. Paul, and singers and dancers from White Earth exhibited their culture. Fairgoers, invited to view indigenous wild rice harvesting techniques, looked in on a live demonstration as an Ojibwe woman parched rice.[20]

During the Depression some Indian people in the western United States joined family camps operated by the Civilian Conservation Corps–Indian Division. The Lakes States Region of the CCC-ID, operated by the Department of the Interior's Office of Indian Affairs, offered relief work to Ojibwe and Dakota people in Minnesota, as well as to Indians in Wisconsin and North Dakota. Minneapolis was the Great Lakes regional headquarters for the CCC-ID, and, not surprisingly, men received most of the paid positions in the emergency relief program. In 1933, shortly after the CCC-ID's national program for American Indians commenced, the corps' first camp in northern Minnesota opened on the Red

Lake Reservation. For the most part, young men over the age of seventeen were recruited to the camps through their agencies; the men then traveled considerable distances in northern Minnesota, separating families, and bunked for weeks at a time in emergency work camps. Men were rotated in and out of jobs to widen the pool of those participating in relief work. The handbook of the CCC-ID suggested subordinate roles for Indian women in poverty relief programs, saying they could serve camp matrons or assist in "recreation and leisure-time activity as will make camp life attractive."[21] Employees received a modest salary of thirty dollars a month; they contributed a small sum for their own food and shelter, and the program dispensed their remaining wages to dependents and relatives. Some workers who lived closer to the work camps lived at home, as did many men from Ojibwe communities at Red Lake, White Earth, Lake Vermilion, and Grand Portage, who were then eligible for a monthly salary of forty-two dollars.

In Michigan, too, there were opportunities for Indian men and women to find work. Camp Marquette opened in 1935 under an agreement between the U.S. Forest Service and the Office of Indian Affairs, employing more than 150 Ojibwe from the Bay Mills community and the Upper Peninsula. Ojibwe workers constructed roads, parks, and fish hatcheries and designed forest and water restoration projects. Camp Marquette had a baseball team and a sweat lodge. The Bay Mills community, which had struggled for decades to have the federal government recognize its sovereignty and treaty rights, found new support from John Collier, the commissioner of Indian Affairs (1933–1945), and his administration. In 1937, the small community held its first election on the reservation, in which Lucy LeBlanc was elected vice president. When the president was called to a position with the Office of Indian Affairs shortly after the election, Lucy became the first Ojibwe woman to serve as a tribal president, perhaps the first American Indian woman to lead a tribe in the modern era.[22]

A small number of Ojibwe women also found employment as social workers for the U.S. Indian Service, investigating the problems of needy Indian families during the Depression. Isabella Robideau, an Ojibwe woman working from the office in Cloquet, Minnesota, held an influential position in the Lake Superior region of Wisconsin and Minnesota, recommending men for hire in CCC-ID work camps and organizing financial arrangements for their dependents. Indian men wrote respectful letters to Robideau seeking her permission to enter work camps. This one came from several men living in Danbury, Wisconsin, written April 6, 1935:

> *Dear Mrs. Robideau,*
>
> *Will you please help us to enter the C.C. camp at Gheen whenever it reopens again? We just have to work in order to live and as you know, no work around here.*
>
> *Please let us know whether it will be open April 15. Also how should we get there?*
>
> > *Yours truly,*
> > *Albert Churchill*
> > *John Dunkley*
> > *William Premo*[23]

Robideau's correspondence displays the confidence with which she meted out advice to camp foremen regarding their employees, on matters including the distribution of men's salaries to their relatives, which meant parents and other adults as well as wives and children. In 1937, she wrote to the agency superintendent regarding the CCC-ID's practice of hiring white men married to Indian women. Her letter suggests that Ojibwe men working for the Fond du Lac CCC-ID mobile unit near Cloquet had circulated a petition favoring the employment of a non-Indian who was a veteran of World War One, "attended council meetings faithfully," drove a "ramshackled car that he takes seven men to work in," and had married Kate Pequette, a Fond du Lac tribal member. The veteran, his wife, and their three tribally enrolled children were all "accepted as an Indian family" and valued as community members.[24] Robideau's correspondence about the Pequettes suggests the fluidity of Ojibwe family life during the Great Depression and the continuing importance to them of kinship and contributing to the common good, rather than their adoption of American concepts of race and blood quantum that characterized the reservation and allotment eras.

In a letter he wrote to the Consolidated Chippewa Agency in 1935, Commissioner John Collier emphasized that "married men with families" be given priority in hiring practices of the CCC-ID.[25] Robideau then explained to her non-Indian colleagues in the CCC-ID that Ojibwe men were very reluctant to leave their homes and families and would do so only as a last resort. At a time during the Depression when "county relief was slim and rather difficult to obtain," Ojibwe men had few alternatives to joining the program to build roads, restore forests, or work on housing projects.[26] Alphonse Caswell, an Ojibwe graduate of the Flandreau Indian School, in South Dakota, watched for forest fires as a WPA employee at home on the Red Lake Reservation. Projects varied at Red Lake, still thick with pine forests, a community that had strategically avoided allotment and retained a substantial communal land base. Workers there cleared fire hazards, cleaned off roadsides, "brushed" truck trails, cut new telephone poles, and improved the stands of forest that stretched over several thousand acres of tribal land. An impressive tree nursery project was in full operation by 1940, along with a project to control a blight of white pine blister rust. Ojibwe artist George Morrison, born along the north shore of Lake Superior near his reservation, began work in the CCC-ID camp in Grand Portage, along with young Indians from across Minnesota—"good healthy work" that encouraged friendship among the people assembled in the camps from a number of Ojibwe communities in the Great Lakes.[27] They lived in barracks, dined communally, and played baseball. In the forests, they attacked the blister rust, pulling diseased white pines out of the ground by their roots.

The landscape around the CCC-ID Nett Lake camp, near the premier wild rice lake, became "a city in miniature," transformed overnight by brown tents in 1933. These gave way to more permanent "neat pine structures, built by Indians with lumber manufactured at the Red Lake Indian saw mill." Emergency conservation workers constructed trails, lookout towers, ranger stations, and telephone lines for more reliable fire detection and control. The camp brought in workers from surrounding Ojibwe communities, including men from White Earth, Leech Lake, Mille Lacs, Fond du Lac, Lake Vermilion, and Grand Portage. In the winter of 1934, a group foreman described the camp at Nett Lake, painting a frigid but bustling scene of activity.

> Far to the north, in the frontier country of Minnesota, close to the Canadian border, the Chippewas of the Nett Lake Indian Emergency Conservation Work Camp on the Bois Fort Reservation, continue their conservation work program, despite sub-zero weather, blinding blizzards and a welter of

deep snow. It is a country where even thermometers freeze. At Christmas time, the thermometer that survived registered fifty-six degrees below. That night, watchmen were kept busy replenishing the fuel in red-hot stoves.[28]

Ojibwe men who worked for the WPA and the CCC-ID still helped their families move to seasonal work sites for harvesting wild rice and making maple sugar. The non-Indian manager of the Nett Lake program was shocked when Ojibwe employees virtually abandoned the camp in August to attend to the wild rice fields; even the better-paid overhead machine operators walked off the job.[29] Remarkably, rather than fire the men for leaving, managers and superintendents decided to permit Ojibwe wild rice gathering in hard times. They then took the further step of taking charge of and "improving" the indigenous harvest. One early project was to upgrade and restore the historic Grand Portage Trail, an important route once used during the fur trade by Indians and the Hudson's Bay Company. The trail had grown over with brush, and Grand Portage harvesters who lived at the arrowhead of Lake Superior could not easily reach their rice lakes. Nett Lake employees also worked to regulate water levels for enhanced wild rice management during 1936.

The Ojibwe wild rice economy became a new focus of emergency relief programs in the Great Lakes region for its potential to be "improved" and "modernized" through government management and the labor of men. Work camp managers, initially unprepared and confounded when the men felt it appropriate to leave work to set up rice camps for their families, soon grew convinced that it was irresponsible to ignore a potential source of income and a natural supply of food for the Ojibwe in years of extreme deprivation. Probably they were unaware of the fact that harvesting wild rice was a predominantly female enterprise, and because the work was conducted outdoors and very labor intensive, it fit within their own cultural categories of men's work. Evidence suggests that the men who made decisions and controlled the labor in federal work programs failed to comprehend, or perhaps simply sidestepped, the issue that must have greatly concerned Ojibwe communities: the traditional wild rice harvest was women's work.

As more men began harvesting wild rice during the Depression, the Ojibwe slowly came to see the work as gender neutral. By the end of World War Two, Ojibwe men clearly dominated the harvesting and production of wild rice in the Great Lakes region. James Mustache, Sr., an indigenous harvester on the Lac Courte Oreilles Reservation, in Wisconsin, who was born around 1903, recalled in late interviews the evolution in wild rice labor that took place during his lifetime. He described his grandmother harvesting wild rice and using burlap sacks for binding material. During the 1930s, men in his community began to harvest rice, and by the latter decades of the twentieth century, few women harvested rice at all at Lac Courte Oreilles.[30]

The patterns Mustache observed taking place at Lac Courte Oreilles were widespread throughout Wisconsin and Minnesota during the Great Depression. It does appear that the original impetus for Ojibwe men to harvest wild rice began with their employment in the poverty relief programs, where they put into operation rice camps in a rational effort to preserve the well-being of their families and communities. The Works Progress Administration, the Indian Division of the Civilian Conservation Corps, and the Minnesota State Forest Service, all of which primarily employed men, helped them establish a new version of wild rice camps to reinvigorate the depressed Ojibwe economy.

In the process, government employers introduced to the harvest their own culture's notions of masculinity, physical labor, and the work ethic. In Minnesota, the State Forest Service encouraged an increasingly male-centered project of wild rice management that emphasized male supervision and masculine industry. Labor that had historically been organized and carried out by large collectives of Ojibwe women was now increasingly tackled by male work crews and even non-Indian managers.[31] The most conspicuous evidence of the entry of Ojibwe men into the harvest during the 1930s was a large-scale project developed when the Minnesota State Forest Service set aside five acres of nontribal land near the Rice River as the Indian Public Wild Rice Camp on the White Earth Reservation, cooperating with the U.S. Indian Service to oversee rice harvesting by permit.

At Rice Lake, Ojibwe men were employed to construct "Indian rice camps" complete with modern conveniences. A report detailed this "modernized" campground, referred to as Project Number One, where hundreds of Ojibwe gathered. After Ojibwe workmen built a new dock across swampy water to the lake, erected six latrines, and thinned aspen and birch trees to open roads to the five-acre wild rice camp, the men began to harvest rice from the lake. In photographs, men in overalls pole boats and knock rice, while the hulling operation also was "a masculine affair."[32] Managers writing to Washington about Project Number One argued that wild rice should continue to be supported with public funds, ending with the comment: "Within the past three years the State of Minnesota has realized the importance of wild rice to the Indians."[33]

Efforts to bolster the wild rice economy in a government-sponsored wild rice campground at White Earth must have seemed ironic to the Ojibwe men and women who experienced the Great Depression. Anyone remotely familiar with recent history would have understood the terrible devastation to the wild rice economy that had recently taken place in Minnesota and Wisconsin. The same government that had for almost a century privileged the timber industry and agriculture over Ojibwe interests to the point of devastating the wild rice environment, and had forced an allotment policy that piece-by-piece undermined Indian land-ownership, now "realized the importance of wild rice to the Indians." For the past fifty years of wild rice habitat decline, the Ojibwe vigorously defended their responsibility of caring for the land and water and their resources. Seemingly overnight, government officials and the State Forest Service in Minnesota yielded to an indigenous economy it had worked for the previous half-century to destroy. The Ojibwe seasonal round came back to life during the Depression, in some places with federal and state endorsement and supervision, to solve the problem of Ojibwe poverty. In another incongruous move, government officials showed instructional photographs at community meetings on the White Earth Reservation to highlight the excellent practices of maple syrup farmers from Vermont. They also suggested the importance of programs to instruct Ojibwe men in the harvesting of maple syrup.[34]

Yet, as the government took charge of organizing the wild rice harvest to solve Ojibwe poverty, it also managed to undercut those efforts by allowing production of wild rice to expand beyond the Ojibwe. The number of non-Indian harvesters and rice buyers multiplied, and the first state regulations of ricing appeared, requiring licenses of all harvesters. Commercial firms and individual buyers soon entered the market, purchasing green wild rice from harvesters, then mechanically processing the grain for sale. When the state of Minnesota began to issue ricing licenses, in 1939, the Ojibwe right to harvest remained protected, but the majority of licenses issued went to individual non-Indians.[35]

The entrance of inexperienced non-Indians into the harvest had dire consequences for both wild rice habitats and Indian economies, as Charles Chambliss, a Washington, D.C., agronomist who studied wild rice, found in the late 1930s.

> During the past eight or ten years there has been a steady growth of whites entering the wild rice beds. They have been greedy and paid no attention to the natural laws regarding the plants' reproduction. As a result many of the better wild rice beds have been ruined by whites gathering the crop in an immature state. The practice of the whites has forced the Indians to gather immature rice. This whole entire practice was ruining the wild rice in Minnesota.[36]

Historians often think of the Great Depression as a time when government officials collaborated with Indian communities to address the terrible problem of Indian poverty and federal work programs were part of a larger effort to rebuild trust.[37] State and federal entities, along with affiliated missionary organizations, had for many years made it a priority to organize the labor of indigenous men and women in ways that conformed to Euro-American notions of female domesticity and male agricultural production. These gender-based attempts to restructure family and community life are associated with misguided "civilization" policies of the previous century, rather than the "Indian New Deal." Yet it is interesting to find that during the 1930s, a dire time when poverty relief work became a necessity for the Ojibwe, federal and state agencies once again embarked on an effort to reshape labor practices, especially as constructed in relation to gender.

The establishment of wild rice campgrounds did represent collaboration with Indian communities, and women and families were not excluded from them. For men, an opportunity to earn a government paycheck to help their families was a great incentive, even though it may have involved a significant change in Ojibwe cultural practices. At the government wild rice camp set up in northern Minnesota, women and children were welcome to wait on shore and take part in processing the harvest while men knocked the rice. It does not appear that Ojibwe people greatly resisted a change that surely amounted to a revolution in their communities. In a time of extreme economic uncertainty, men joined women as active harvesters of wild rice, moving into the gendered spaces where Ojibwe women sang harvesting songs and labored together in support of their families and a rich community life.

The WPA state guide to Minnesota blithely pronounced in its 1938 publication, "The most hopeful indication of the possible economic redemption of the Chippewa is their growing awareness of the advantages of group effort."[38] Given the history of the Ojibwe in the Great Lakes region, who regarded family and group labor (much of it involving separate male and female collectives) as the essence of community life, such a statement demonstrates pointedly how little government entities truly understood about the indigenous people whose lives they presumed to reshape. The guide was simply referring to the arrival of a new wild rice cooperative on the Leech Lake Ojibwe Reservation in northern Minnesota that opened in 1934.

Today many sell their products through the recently founded Chippewa Co-operative Marketing Association, which began with a capital of $100,000 from the tribal treasury. It not only insures the craftsman a better price for his wares, but also sponsors a wild rice cleaning and packing factory designed to replace the primitive harvesting and cleaning methods still used by Indians in the north woods. Eventually the making and marketing of maple sugar will be added to the co-operative's undertakings.[39]

Photographs of Ojibwe people harvesting rice are a useful means of tracking changes in the work of men and women, and it is obvious that men grew more active in the enterprise during and after the Great Depression. Through the years until the present day, women are pictured harvesting rice with family members or husbands, though female collectives ceased to exist.

In 1934 the Ojibwe established a wild rice cooperative in northern Minnesota. Co-op members, primarily from Leech Lake but also from White Earth, could vote and share in any dividends that resulted. The cooperative elected officers and paid wages directly to harvesters who brought in rice. The manager of the cooperative was Paul LaRoque, an Ojibwe man from Beaulieu, Minnesota, who also served as rice buyer, paying out amounts that varied annually from fifteen thousand to thirty thousand dollars to purchase finished wild rice from Ojibwe harvesters.[40] The Indian agency in northern Minnesota purchased wild rice from the co-op to supply food for relief cases in the native community.[41] Letters from the co-op show that LaRoque corresponded with a wide range of individuals and businesses, from D'Arcy McNickle, the Flathead employee of the Bureau of Indian Affairs in Washington, to the managers of the Curtis Hotel in Minneapolis, who also purchased Ojibwe-harvested rice. LaRoque answered everyone who wrote to the co-op, and he diligently promoted wild rice in Minnesota and throughout the United States.

Dear Mrs. Skifstrom:
You are the winner of the Wild Rice Guessing contest, which was
held in Bemidji during the Paul Bunyan Carnival, your guess
being 12,600 and the correct figure was 12,576 kernels. Your 5 lbs.
of No. 1 wild rice is being shipped to you today.

> *Sincerely yours,*
> *Paul LaRoque, Manager*
> *Wild Rice Corporate Enterprise*

Mr. D'Arcy McNickle
C/o Indian Office
Washington, D.C.
February 8, 1940

Dear Mr. McNickle:
Thank you kindly for your order of five pounds of No.1 Wild Rice.
Your order was shipped out yesterday afternoon. The charges are
listed below:

5 lbs. wild rice @ 45¢:	*$2.25*
Postage:	*.47*
	$2.72

Your check or Money Order should be made payable to Paul
LaRoque, Manager, Wild Rice Corporate Enterprise.
We will be glad to fill any other wild rice orders you may have
at any time.

> *Sincerely yours,*
> *Paul LaRoque, Manager*
> *Wild Rice Corporate Enterprise*

The co-op's records show that, despite the shift in gendered
labor, women were active in the organization and retained a foothold

in the wild rice economy.[42] Three women referred to by name in the co-op records, Mrs. Kate Nelson, Mrs. Lovelace, and Mrs. Broker, and one other unnamed Ojibwe woman, were important harvesters for the cooperative in the late 1930s, and the co-op delivered barrels to all four women for parching rice. The cooperative described the rice it sold to the public as "parched, finished, and graded under careful and expert supervision," a testimonial to the practiced skills of its Ojibwe women participants. One of these, Cecelia Rock, managed the cooperative during the early 1940s, but perhaps this position may have been temporary due to the absence of Ojibwe men during the war years.

Gedakaakoons, a young Ojibwe who helped market rice for the cooperative, was photographed in her jingle dress, amid Ojibwe handicrafts made by women, in the co-op's log warehouse on the Leech Lake Reservation.[43] The image shows her holding a bag of wild rice that pictures a drum with feathers. In her outfit, she greatly resembles one of her Minnesota commercial contemporaries, the "Indian Maiden" pictured since 1928 on Land O'Lakes dairy cartons. Land O'Lakes is an old Minneapolis–St. Paul company, also a cooperative. The Ojibwe wild rice cooperative may have appropriated the maiden for their own advertising purposes in the 1930s, from a regional company that had recently appropriated this image from Indians in Minnesota.[44] That an Ojibwe cooperative employed an "Indian Maiden" in their modest marketing campaign was not a sign of the demise of Ojibwe women as active harvesters but, rather, a creative adoption of an already popular image of Indian womanhood. The cooperative lasted a decade, surviving the Depression but not World War Two, and closed in 1944.

Women continued to harvest wild rice with their families in other areas of the Great Lakes region. In 1939, the year Minnesota harvesters were required to purchase ricing licenses, a number of women harvested rice at Portage Lake and Perch Lake in central

Minnesota, contending with non-Indian harvesters who had picked rice that was too green and a game warden who had forced Indians off the lakes. Despite harassment, one woman reported an increase in her harvest over that of the previous year, when water levels were low, bringing in four hundred pounds of green rice.[45] Some Ojibwe women applied for licenses to harvest wild rice, including Naomi Warren LaDue of White Earth, who complained of a long trip to Bemidji to pay her fee to the game warden.[46]

Ricing licenses, new methods of processing rice, non-Indian harvesters, commercial buyers, and the introduction of government wild rice campgrounds deeply influenced Ojibwe labor practices associated with the harvest in the years following the Depression. Once again, indigenous women adapted, preserving the fundamental structures of Ojibwe society by working with the wild rice cooperative at Leech Lake and ricing by state permit when that became a requirement. They continued to harvest wild rice, laboring alongside other women and an increasing number of male relatives, in the 1930s and 1940s, though by 1940 they were no longer a majority.

A new population invaded the lakes in postwar America, building summer homes and new economies around tourism while advancing popular ideas of leisure and landscapes of recreation—a lifestyle that continues to ravage land, water, and their resources. The Ojibwe have never ceased their efforts to legally protect wild rice, and today the opening of the wild rice season is determined by the Great Lakes Indian Fish and Wildlife Commission, a consortium of Ojibwe tribes.[47] Indigenous approaches to wild rice management clash with the interests of the biotechnology industry and some university researchers over the genetic engineering of wild rice. The Ojibwe persist in taking responsibility for caring for *manoomin*, dedicated to the survival and integrity of a uniquely perfect grain that once sustained whole communities.

5

MOUNT PLEASANT

Metaphor of the Muskrat

THE INDIAN BOARDING SCHOOL that opened at Mount Pleasant, Michigan, in 1893 was erected on sacred homelands, a place where the Anishinaabeg had for generations buried their dead. During the forty years of the school's operation, children who occupied it at times felt unsettled, because their living quarters, classrooms, and workstations covered the burial grounds and they noticed unusual noises in the buildings and on campus. The government school encompassed 320 acres, on land formerly part of the Isabella Reservation. Among its thirty buildings, mostly constructed of brick, were administrative offices, classrooms, student dormitories, employee cottages, barns, and a school hospital. The Chippewa River runs through Mount Pleasant, which was a predominantly non-Indian town by the time the school opened, though a small Ojibwe community survived. Some of Mount Pleasant's story can be told through photographs. In one picture, girls pose in several rows before a small bridge on campus. They each have carefully arranged hair and, except for one child, somber faces. A girl of about thirteen at the edge of the photograph stands with hands clasped in front of her dress and smiles gently into the camera. Another image shows a class of eight older teenagers, or "big girls" as they were called, wearing ruffled white caps and aprons over long dresses, standing dutifully next to their domestic science teacher. Her job was to prepare them for employment as house servants and maids. They and other students at Mount Pleasant liked to tell stories of the *jiibayag*, or ghosts, that roamed their school.[1]

Historians generally conceive of the boarding school era as the half-century beginning with the founding of the Indian Industrial School at Carlisle, Pennsylvania, in 1879 and ending around 1940, after the Great Depression. Schools that continued after that time did not share the same initial objective of cultural assimilation. In the 1930s, the policymakers and reformers of the Indian New Deal piloted a significant trend toward public school education, and dozens of boarding schools like Mount Pleasant closed. For fifty years, though, boarding school education was predominant, and in 1899, twenty-five schools in fifteen states had a total population of twenty thousand American Indian children. Ojibwe students attended schools in the Great Lakes region that included Hayward, Tomah, Pipestone, Flandreau, and Mount Pleasant, and some went farther away to Haskell or Carlisle. In Carlisle's final year of operation, 1917, Ojibwe students were in the majority among a highly diverse student body composed of fifty-eight tribes.[2]

Compulsory school attendance laws aimed at American Indian children were first passed by Congress in the early 1890s and left families with few alternatives to an education for "civilization." In 1898, at the urging of Commissioner of Indian Affairs William Jones, a new law was passed, further empowering the government to remove children from their homes and place them in schools. During the next several years, boarding schools grew increasingly overcrowded as school officials and Indian agents worked to fill them to capacity. Children were drafted to recruit for the schools. In a rather extreme example from 1900, an Ojibwe boy named Simon Bonga enlisted six other Ojibwe children, one right out of the reservation school at Leech Lake, in northern Minnesota; brought them to the agency doctor for a physical; and, "without the consent of their parents," took them to boarding school. Even the Indian agent found the "whole proceeding was very irregular" and stated that, "while I have universally extended courtesies to this school and to all others, I think this is going a little too far."[3]

Force and intimidation were among the methods used to separate children from their families; this might involve withholding rations and annuities or simply taking children to school against parental wishes. Canadian officials resorted to similar measures. One important Ojibwe author, Basil Johnston, described his own story of being taken from his rural home on the Cape Croker Reserve in Ontario to attend a residential school during the 1930s, along with a four-year-old sister. In his memoir, *Indian School Days*, he recalled in painstaking detail the callousness of this event and the dismayed reaction of his mother and grandmother when the Indian agent threatened to take all the children in the family to boarding school if they failed to comply with his quota of two children. As Johnston explained, "The Indian agent knew how to handle Indians, especially Indian women."[4]

It was not uncommon for siblings or cousins to jointly attend boarding school. Brother and sister Ranee and George Teeple, of the Bay Mills community, entered boarding school together as young children. These strikingly beautiful children stood in their Mount Pleasant uniforms for a photograph around 1900, the older sister in an Edwardian sailor suit and a velvet hat.[5] Bay Mills Ojibwe had attended Catholic and other local missionary schools prior to Mount Pleasant, and literacy rates were high among

Michigan Indians at the beginning of the boarding school era.[6] For most children the initial trip to boarding school was their first experience leaving home. For two generations in the United States and longer in Canada, surviving boarding school became part of a broader, pan-indigenous experience.

Indian boarding schools across the United States had much in common with Mount Pleasant in that all followed the model set by the Indian Industrial School at Carlisle, the most prominent school. Carlisle's founder was a former officer in the U.S. military, Richard Henry Pratt. Pratt was the architect of the austere boarding school program and the creator of the "outing program," which required students to spend half the day in the classroom and the remainder in manual labor around the school. Boarding schools adopted Pratt's core curriculum and his attitude that Indian children needed to learn to adapt to Euro-American civilization at the expense of their own culture. The outing program was meant to expose young people to American culture through their labor. Outing students, especially in the summer, worked as farmhands and domestic servants.

Mount Pleasant was a typical Indian boarding school in an era when such institutions were a means for the U.S. government to restructure indigenous gender roles. The girls at Mount Pleasant worked in the school's kitchens and laundry rooms in a home economics–based curriculum that prepared them for a future as maids and cooks or as wives in thrifty households. Their hard work of cleaning, washing clothes, sewing and mending linen and uniforms, cooking and baking for the school and its employees—all essential labor for the operation of the school—was considered the foundation of their vocational training. There were dormitories at Mount Pleasant for both younger and older girls, who spent long days in the classroom or at work. The curriculum and the campus were geared toward agricultural production, with gardens, barns, and a dairy herd.

Mount Pleasant was an orderly campus not without small charms, including a pond, a gymnasium, and a well-kept playground. Pictures from early in the century show young girls in below-the-knee dresses playing on slides, teeter-totters, climbers, and swings. Other images portray teams of handsome older boys in athletic uniforms playing football and standing together holding baseball gloves. The emphasis on sports to an extent followed white subscription to stereotypes about indigenous peoples. As the commissioner of Indian Affairs, Francis E. Leupp, stated, "I like the Indian for what is in him. I want to see his splendid inherited physique kept up, because he glories like his ancestors in fresh air, in freedom, in activities, and in feats of strength."[7] Sports were exceptionally popular at Indian boarding schools, and evidence suggests that athletes had their own interpretations of their value, apart from conforming to white authorities' views of their physicality.[8]

School records indicate that more than half the student body at Mount Pleasant was Ojibwe, the second-largest group Ottawa, with smaller numbers of Potawatomi and other children. Paradoxically, boarding school reunited the Anishinaabeg youth. In 1925, the school's 411 students were described by Mount Pleasant's superintendent as children who wore "modern attire" and "spoke English, and could read and write in English." The indigenous people of Michigan and their children at school were both tribally and ethnically diverse, according to the superintendent, who further explained that "intermarriage with the whites and negroes has gone on for generations." For most years of its operation, Mount Pleasant educated children through eighth grade, though in 1927 the school introduced a ninth grade and dropped the first grade "in accordance with the growing belief that boarding schools are not the best place for young children."[9]

There is no single narrative of the boarding school experience. Students had the potential to be happy or miserable, thriving or sick, skilled or untrained. Some found a caring home, while others despised their teachers and everything about their environment. Yet by the 1930s, changing ideas about race in America and the move away from assimilation created positive institutional change throughout the Indian education system, both on and off the reservation. To appreciate the complexity of the experience, it is tremendously important to consider the wide range of reasons Ojibwe and other children attended boarding schools. Not every story is one of children ripped from parents' arms by government forces. Many students had a very real desire to learn English, play in the school band, or, for some adolescents, get away from their parents. Students could be very enthusiastic about athletic programs.[10] Families also sought out vocational training and schooling for their children. Indeed, the federal archives are full of letters from Ojibwe and other families seeking to enroll their children in the boarding schools. For decades, these institutions presented the only opportunity for Ojibwe children to gain an education, as public school integration was a slow struggle for American Indians.

The Mount Pleasant school superintendent explained the increasing landlessness of Michigan Ojibwe in a letter written the year the school opened, but he refuted an assumption that Indians in his state relied exclusively on the dole, despite their poverty.

As a general rule the Indians of Michigan are in the same political and economic status as the average white citizen. They vote, pay taxes and earn their living by the sweat of their brows. They receive no aid from the Government since they have no connection other than a sentimental one. Formerly all heads of families belonging to the Saginaw Swan Creek and Black River bands were given allotments of land averaging about 40 acres, but much of this has passed from Indian ownership and as a result the average Michigan Indian makes his living by labor.[11]

Still, by and large, poverty is the greatest explanation for why students in the United States attended government boarding schools after assimilation no longer dominated federal policy. A social worker at Mount Pleasant described an extraordinarily hardworking Ojibwe people in Michigan in 1932, still unable to support their families:

One of our serious problems with Indian families in Michigan is poverty. Many of the families own land and raise their own food supply. Others support themselves and families as best they can by any kind of laboring work they can get. They depend a good deal on natural resources. In the berry-picking season, Indian families are to be found picking berries and selling them. Just now they are "frogging." They also fish in certain parts of the state and ship their fish to Chicago. In cherry season, they pick cherries, and then work in the canneries if they have a chance. In this part of the state they work in the beet fields during the summer. Lumbering is a common winter occupation. The making of splint baskets and porcupine quill baskets are about the only Indian arts that are practiced extensively. Some of the Indian women make very beautiful baskets; others are less skillful in their work. The income from these baskets is sometimes all there is to support an Indian family during the winter. As you can see, none of these occupations is a source of regular stated income and therefore many of the families have to live a hand to mouth existence. The problem of clothing the family is much more difficult than that of feeding them; and often the reason that children are kept out of school in the winter is that they do not have warm enough clothing to protect them from the cold. [12]

There were constant symptoms of fracture and despair in Ojibwe community life throughout the boarding school era. One of the most troubling signs of community instability was the large number of orphaned children and of extended families who were unable to care for them. Ojibwe society had always embraced dependent children, and families commonly included children who were adopted. In the early twentieth century, this arrangement slowly changed when impoverished Ojibwe communities began to rely on boarding schools to care for dependent children. As the superintendent of Mount Pleasant wrote in a letter, the students "who attend this school are for the most part children from broken homes, orphans or those who live too far from public schools."[13] Still, the more frequent enrollments did not mean that the bonds of community had been totally shattered. There are countless examples of boarding school students being reared by single parents, grandparents, or aunts and uncles. In cases where children were orphaned and eventually put under the care of boarding schools, even teenagers living on their own who attended the schools after the death of a parent or relative, records indicate that they were still part of Ojibwe communities and cared about by family members at home.

Grandparents and other family members filled an indispensable role when parents died. Dawn Woman, the widowed wife of

Marksman interviewed in the WPA project, lived to see her great-grandchildren attend government boarding schools. Her daughter, Mary Twobirds of the Bad River Reservation, became the caretaker of several grandchildren when her own daughter died in the 1920s. Twobirds summed up her situation: "I am the guardian of these poor children since their mother died" and "I've worked hard to raise these children on my own." She was as determined as her own widowed mother had been in the face of tragedy years before, and she diligently kept the family together. She owned a secondhand car, but winters in northern Wisconsin often prevented the twelve-mile drive into Ashland for public school, so sending her grandchildren to the Flandreau boarding school in South Dakota became an opportunity for them to graduate.[14]

The fracture of Ojibwe family and social networks in the post-allotment Great Lakes meant that some children slipped through the cracks. That a number of young people were lost to Ojibwe communities during the boarding school era is also not surprising, given the personal histories of individual students. Some had parents who wasted away in tuberculosis sanitariums or suffered mental illness. Disease, high rates of adult mortality, disability, and the overriding struggle with poverty overwhelmed the resources of kin networks and day-to-day life, offering a grim portrait of the social history of reservations and Ojibwe communities in the early twentieth century.

Regardless of the circumstances that landed students in government boarding school, they invariably experienced a profound homesickness after their arrival. The problem was exacerbated because boarding school life was designed as an experiment in cultural isolation and alienation. Often, parents were stripped of the power to make decisions for their child's well-being, and school officials were designated as the final authority on child welfare and home visits. Ojibwe mothers constantly collided with administrators over the emotional health of their children, revealing a deep cultural divide over ideas regarding mental and emotional health and the body. Women interpreted homesickness and longing for family as an authentic problem, one to be remedied when it emerged in children, but it was continually dismissed as insignificant by officials. The problem of homesickness was aggravated because boarding schools expected students to continue their programs for a term of study that generally lasted four years, during which time they were supposed to remain at school. Prevailing assumptions about American Indian cultural assimilation theorized that keeping students away from the influence of family and community was the best way to effect change, and administrators enforced school rules with rigor.

One Wisconsin Ojibwe mother, trying to reunite with her daughter after she had been away to boarding school for four years during the 1920s, wrote plaintively to the administrator that "I know she will feel more like going to school next fall if she sees her folks once more." Her daughter was the impetus behind a small campaign of letters the woman wrote to the superintendent, pleading with him to send "her home to me for a few weeks" and literally begging "just to see her before she goes to school again." Discouraged, the mother appealed to the Indian agent at Lac Courte Oreilles but found absolutely no support there. He wrote back with only a curt message, saying nothing "would justify me sending her home."[15] This attitude on the part of administrators so incensed a mother from Red Lake that she wrote to her daughter's superintendent with the scathing observation, "It seems it would be much easier to get her out of prison than out of your school."[16]

Indian boarding schools were funded on a per capita basis, so officials were encouraged by the budget increase for salaries and schools that came with upping their enrollment. However, boarding schools and Indian agencies very soon reported an increase in epidemic disease. Agents and superintendents created a hazardous and sometimes deadly environment for children by recklessly enrolling sick children along with healthy students.[17] The possibility of contracting trachoma or tuberculosis, the dual plague of government boarding schools, loomed large as a threat to children's health in most schools. Trachoma was a terribly infectious eye disease that became chronic in boarding school children before the advent of sulfa drugs in the late 1930s. It was painful and included the potential of lifelong damage as inflamed eyelids turned inward, resulting in scratches to the delicate cornea. Transmitted similar to the less harmful conjunctivitis, trachoma was spread by the common use of towels and water in boarding schools, where communal practices were the standard. As early as 1912, public health officials identified the widening trachoma epidemic on reservations as being spread by students returning home from government boarding schools, and the problem of disability and blindness was widespread.[18]

Tuberculosis was an incurable disease during the boarding school era, killing half of all children who developed it after a period of illness and suffering. Some Ojibwe children with tuberculosis were shipped to the school sanitariums that had opened by 1915, or the Sac and Fox Sanatorium for children and adults in Iowa. Others stayed in school or reservation hospitals; significant numbers of sick children went home, either to die or to recover their health in the company of the people they loved. In the United States, indigenous people who developed tuberculosis were generally segregated into Indian tuberculosis sanitariums rather than institutions established for whites, or even separate Indian wings of integrated state sanitariums, such as Ah Gwah Ching in northern

Minnesota. As the cemeteries at Carlisle, Haskell, and other schools attest, some young people were buried at boarding school.

Tuberculosis could attack the lungs or other body systems, and boarding school students sometimes hemorrhaged from the lungs or experienced tubercular-related body sores. An implausibly resilient young Bad River Ojibwe girl named Harriet, who had contracted tuberculosis, advocated for her own health and future when she wrote to her school superintendent in 1924, explaining her painful lesions and asking him the pointed question, "How do you expect me to learn and study when I suffer so?" Harriet, who had the support of her parents regarding her wish to enter a sanitarium, summarized her dilemma: "Would you rather have me go away to a sanatorium and get well quicker and where I can learn and be happy or, Have me going to school and suffer."[19]

Ojibwe daughters grew up accustomed to enjoying the seasonal round of work shared with other women; by contrast, the daily routine of boarding schools stressed authority and disciplined labor. The Mount Pleasant handbook from 1917–18 illustrates the boarding school curriculum for girls: The day was long, beginning with a rising bell and reveille at 5:30 a.m., and ending with taps and lights-out at 9 p.m. The girls had domestic science training every schoolday from 7:30 in the morning until 6:30 in the evening, with reference made to changing times for "serving days," related to work in the dining room. Time was set aside Monday for calisthenics for older girls and games and songs for the younger group. Wednesday was for marching and exercise, and students took part in a "Large Boys and Girls Social" between 7 and 9:30 p.m. on alternating Friday evenings.

Ojibwe families raised daughters to be self-reliant at an early age, and first menstruation served as an intrinsic sign not just of growing physical maturity but of their ability to handle new social responsibilities. Yet this social growth was discouraged in boarding schools. Mount Pleasant carefully supervised girls, especially those past puberty, who were permitted to go to town one Saturday morning each month only for shopping and only with a chaperone. Older girls in the sixth, seventh, and eighth grades took part in literary society meetings, had some first-aid training, and listened to lectures on hygiene and health. In 1917, the school nurse initiated a series of "Save the Baby" lectures, popular in the early twentieth century, where girls learned about pregnancy, infant care, and breast and bottle feeding. This included lectures on childhood illness with an emphasis on "sanitation of homes where infants reside, with special reference to tuberculosis and trachoma." In addition, the handbook noted that "each girl will be required, before graduation, to present a complete layette made by herself, according to a lecture given October 30, 1917."[20]

Every single federally funded boarding school in the United States regarded Christianity as essential to the mission of civilization. There was no mention of Anishinaabe spiritual beliefs in the handbook, but there was a school chapel at Mount Pleasant where "undenominational" children attended Christian services. The superintendent described students as "evenly divided between the Catholics and Protestants" and wrote that their "religious education here is well cared for by our local pastors." Students regarded as Catholic were given classroom instruction every Saturday afternoon by nuns from the local parochial school. Methodism was the dominant Christian faith at the Bay Mills community, and students of that denomination went to Sunday school at the Methodist Episcopal Church in Mount Pleasant.[21]

The U.S. Indian School at Mount Pleasant patriotically maintained a special honor roll of its former students who had served in the army or navy. The list was long for 1917–18, an era of heavy U.S.

involvement in World War One. During the war, Indian boarding school students exchanged one uniform for another in great numbers, as sixteen thousand American Indians left home to serve. The small school's honor roll recognized sixty former students who had joined the military even prior to the 1924 Indian Citizenship Act, which at long last conceded this symbol of union in American society to all Indians. Most Michigan Ojibwe were already citizens by 1924, and boarding school students and graduates who spoke English and were classified as U.S. citizens became the easiest target of war recruitment efforts among American Indians.

Volunteer rates were higher from boarding schools than from Indian reservations, as the schools celebrated military culture. Ojibwe communities were known to question practices that required men to register for the selective service as a violation of tribal sovereignty. The high turnout of Indian students, and Indians in general, in the American forces of World War One foreshadowed the remarkable response of Indian men and women to World War Two, when men were eligible for the draft.

Despite the conformity and obedience boarding schools required, students could be remarkably defiant. Rebellions were large and small, public and deeply personal. Students at the Haskell boarding school in Kansas rioted during a school event in 1919, and a number of them were later expelled. Older girls in the outing program at Haskell during the 1930s, often working in local households in Lawrence or Kansas City, were highly spirited domestic servants: they smoked, stayed out late, had boyfriends, bribed children in the family not to snitch on them, and carried on like teenagers in every way possible.[22] Basil Johnston's tender memoir of child life in his Ontario residential school brilliantly captures the spirit of the everyday weapons powerless students creatively used to resist the authority of the Jesuits who operated his institution.[23] His classmates elevated the leisurely act of "dawdling," which completely frustrated teachers, to a fine art.

It is poignant that Indian students in government boarding schools became "runaways" or "deserters," as they were called by officials, simply to spend time with their families and loved ones at home. Mount Pleasant and some of the other schools in the Great Lakes region had fairly high numbers of runaways. Indian Commissioner Charles Rhoads offered a rather humane perspective on the problem to the staff of Mount Pleasant, saying that they must simply show "human sympathy and companionship" and that "the school should be made as interesting and full of adventure as life on the outside, this is not impossible."[24] Still, boarding school students who missed their families and could not afford the expense of train travel, or those who simply wished to avoid the painfully paternalistic and numbing bureaucratic rituals involved in gaining formal permission to go home, often just skipped town. Boys could more easily run away undetected because they had more autonomy than girls, who were always carefully chaperoned by faculty and staff when they were off campus. Even so, Ojibwe student Mary Badboy still held "the run away record for the year" at Flandreau in 1933.[25]

The practice of keeping children at boarding school for appalling lengths of time relaxed once policymakers decided the boarding school concept was obsolete, the prevailing opinion in Washington during the 1930s. It was a transitional moment in Indian education, defined by the closure of dozens of the boarding schools, including Mount Pleasant in 1933, and the shift toward public school education, though boarding school enrollment remained high through the 1930s due to the effect of the Depression.

In June of 1933 a letter arrived at Mount Pleasant addressed to a student named Julius Anse, of Suttons Bay, Michigan. Ten days before, Commissioner of Indian Affairs John Collier had received a letter from the worried Julius, who had written directly to Washington expressing concern about arrangements for Indian children like him who were headed to public school once Mount Pleasant closed. In what must have been a golden age of correspondence within the agency, Collier himself responded to Julius' letter to clarify issues related to the public school attendance of students enrolled at Mount Pleasant. Collier wrote:

> We pay tuition to public schools for the attendance of pupils in districts where the circumstances warrant. We do not pay for students who have less than one-quarter Indian blood, nor for the children of taxpaying Indians. You ask that you be permitted to go to the Traverse City School instead of either of the two high schools near your home. This is a matter which will be left to the public school officials, and it will probably be necessary for you to attend the high school maintained for your district. We are sending copies of your letter and our reply to Superintendent Christy who will refer your case to Miss Cheney who has charge of the matter of placing the Mount Pleasant Indian children in public schools.[26]

When Mount Pleasant ended its mission to educate Indians in Michigan, most teenagers transferred to high school at Haskell or Flandreau, rather than to public school. "Since then only fifty orphaned children have been kept in the dormitories," wrote the superintendent in 1933, and "they are attending the city grade and high school." Even those students were soon fostered out to boarding homes at the expense of the federal government.[27] Some students returned to local schools in their communities. Ojibwe and several non-Indian students at Bay Mills attended a rural school in "a building in a very dilapidated state," with a "broken, rough, and uneven floor." It was a small school with just one teacher, but despite its simplicity, Bay Mills students almost never missed class during the year 1934.[28] The former Indian boarding school at Mount Pleasant was turned over to another institution, and plans were drawn to bring mentally disabled boys to the campus. The school property that held burial grounds and once belonged to the Ojibwe of the Isabella Reservation was transferred to the state of Michigan.

In the early 1990s a reunion was held in the Saginaw Ojibwe community for surviving students of the U.S. Indian School at Mount Pleasant. Ojibwe, Ottawa, and Potawatomi elders who had attended Mount Pleasant between 1910 and 1933 took part in the gathering. The twenty or so alumni talked about their memories of the school, which were both good and bad. They laughed as they remembered the student culture, the crushes and boyfriends, and the simple pleasures of modern plumbing, regular meals, and a school community of boys and girls who were like one big family. When asked to tell something of his experience, one elder recollected, "If it wasn't for this school, I would've starved to death." The elders sadly recalled the reasons that brought them to school, which was in most cases the death of a mother. As Isabella Langton remarked, "My mother was dying and she put me in boarding school. The only thing I didn't like was they didn't let you talk Indian." They grew somber as they recalled the small children who cried at night, and as they listened to an elderly Ojibwe man's story of going to school after authorities in Marquette, Michigan, decided that his deaf parents should not raise him. He also remembered his school beatings, inflicted with a rubber hose. These people had been survivors since childhood.[29]

The history of American Indian boarding schools in the United States contains an underlying narrative that provides remarkable detail about the struggles of a newly impoverished and dispossessed people for the basic necessities of life and about the determined efforts of the powerful against the powerless. There is a haunting legacy to this history, because it involved not just the authority of the American government over the sovereignty of Indian nations but also adult authority in the face of child vulnerability. In the final analysis, like other chapters of Indian–U.S. relations, the boarding school history is also a narrative about the desire for control over indigenous land and resources, which gave rise to the institution, since the boarding school concept was politically motivated by the allotment of Indian reservations. Reformers and politicians laid claim to an idea of the Indian community as obsolete, guided by their principle that Indians must adopt values of individualism and be citizens and agricultural or industrial workers since they could no longer afford a life of caring for their land and resources. Indian boarding schools were a unique form of segregated education to emerge in the history of the United States and, like other forms of segregation, served the interests of a white majority.

6

MINNEAPOLIS

A Renaissance of Spirit

WORLD WAR Two hastened the mobility of Ojibwe people, who became part of a nationwide social movement that would relocate nearly 80 percent of the American Indian population to cities by the end of the twentieth century. The war took on added resonance since the Indian Citizenship Act of 1924 ensured that all eligible men might be drafted, deploying young soldiers from rural reservation communities to the battle zones of distant lands. It motivated men and women to leave behind the worst aspects of reservation poverty and opened doors to new opportunities, especially in defense and other wartime industries and jobs that arose due to shortages. Ojibwe women left home to work as army nurses, or to serve elsewhere in the armed forces. Minneapolis and surrounding metropolitan counties, especially the city's Phillips neighborhood, became a center for Indian population growth and community connections even before the U.S. government initiated the Urban Relocation Program of the 1950s. Those who stayed on in the city found other Indians, and a kinship was forged among peoples who shared cultural bonds and a common history of colonialism and pain inflicted in the form of boarding schools, assimilation, and the loss of land. Ignatia Broker, one of the Ojibwe from White Earth who arrived in Minneapolis during the war, described the urban solidarity of nations as "an island from which a revival of spirit began."[1] Minneapolis was home to a new generation, living in cities and interacting within an expansive network of tribes and identities.

World War Two represented a time of tremendous change for American Indians, and one can imagine an abrupt end to one way of life and the beginning of a modern, urban reality for those transplanted to the city. Yet despite facing new and difficult conditions outside the reservation, the many who left consistently found ways to create community and preserve family ties. Migrating Ojibwe women gathered with relatives and friends and exchanged information. In postwar cities, they acted in response to the growing needs of their families and other Indian people by developing new ideas about labor, but they did so in unique ways that linked the values of the traditional Ojibwe economy to the city. Rather than abandon cultural ideas about work, women reimagined and reshaped their labor in ways that were of greatest worth to the Indian community.

In 1900, the Ojibwe population was overwhelmingly rural and reservation-based, but as it rebounded in the mid-twentieth century it became more urban with each passing decade. World War Two allowed some Ojibwe women to gain a foothold in the city because of the prospect of wartime employment; later, the GI Bill provided other incentives to returning soldiers and their families. The controversial postwar termination and relocation policies of the federal government encouraged further American Indian resettlement in cities. In the 1950s and 1960s, conservatives in the U.S. Congress moved to "terminate" federal responsibility and financial support to Indian tribes, abandon treaty responsibilities, and sponsor the movement of Indian people into cities. The policy was a disaster for tribes terminated early on, and the Ojibwe at North Dakota's Turtle Mountains were slated for termination until the example of the Menominee of Wisconsin turned into an unmitigated catastrophe. Termination immediately destabilized Indian economies and lowered standards of health. Once termination ended, in the early 1970s, the urban Indian population of Minneapolis and its metropolitan counties exceeded that in almost any other American city. The 1990 U.S. Census was considered a landmark for revealing that slightly more than half of the American Indian population lived in urban areas.[2] The census also indicated an Ojibwe population of 103,826 (not including the Canadian Ojibwe population of approximately the same size), making the Ojibwe the third-largest tribal group in the United States, after the Navajo and the Cherokee. Twenty-first-century census estimates revealed an even larger Indian population in cities.[3]

The Ojibwe in the upper Midwest struggled for physical and cultural survival in the aftermath of the post-allotment looting of reservations, and they found their land base dwindling from the ravages of timber companies and other land sharks who systematically swindled Ojibwe allotments across the Great Lakes region, from Bay Mills to White Earth. Another predator was the county tax office, which illegally seized countless Ojibwe allotments. The loss of tribal homelands touched off the urban migration that continued for most of the twentieth century. Nationally, statistics make plain the decline in tribal land-ownership. The allotment of reservations formally ended in 1934, during the administration of Franklin D. Roosevelt, a time when American Indians were reduced to ownership of 48 million acres of homeland, down from the 138 million they possessed in 1887.[4]

Once Ojibwe people were dispossessed of their best land for hunting, fishing, and gathering, the formerly dependable seasonal economy languished in the Great Lakes region. Problems of poor nutrition, disability, and disease arose, which further compromised Ojibwe lives and livelihoods in the communities. By the Great Depression, opportunities for wage work in lumber camps and border towns dried up, and despite the efforts of the CCC-ID, steady employment remained difficult to find. World War Two would introduce a variety of new economic opportunities for the Ojibwe, and real job prospects in nearby cities encouraged migration even before the emergence of the federally sponsored relocation programs. In this complex setting, in the face of these many challenges, men departed for wars, and thousands of Ojibwe men and women migrated to cities in search of jobs.

Minneapolis, St. Paul, and Duluth were popular destinations for Ojibwe people. Women from the plundered White Earth Reservation, a community reduced to poverty and near-landlessness, had begun migrating to Minneapolis as early as the 1920s, but their numbers increased greatly during the war years. Some already mothers, these women found jobs in the city and often switched employers or moved in response to changing opportunities. Their participation in the urban labor force was motivated by an array of family and community priorities. Before the growth of a sizable Indian community in postwar Minneapolis and St. Paul, life could be lonely for young women in the city. In one example from 1924, a young mother, during breaks from long days working in the linen room at the Ryan Hotel in downtown St. Paul, wrote letters to her three sons at boarding school as she worked toward their future together in the Twin Cities.[5]

Ojibwe women formed personal networks with other Indian people that were essential to their survival in the city. Their early efforts were an expression of indigenous values that resulted in the emergence of distinctive urban Indian communities in the Great

Lakes region. One leader, Emily Peake, was from a White Earth family that had come to Minneapolis, where she was born in 1920 and later began school. During World War Two, she worked at Honeywell, making parachutes, before joining the Women's Coast Guard in 1944. She attended the University of Minnesota on the GI Bill, graduating in 1947. Peake and friends formed an early social club for native women during the 1940s in an effort that presaged later significant Indian organizations and centers of community life. After spending time working in Europe, Peake returned to Minneapolis, and during the termination era she helped found the Upper Midwest American Indian Center with Dakota and Ojibwe colleagues.

One of these colleagues was Winnie Jourdain, a young widow with a four-year-old son, who came to Minneapolis from White Earth in 1926. Like Emily Peake, Jourdain was a key figure in the establishment of the early urban Indian community. For the next several decades, she and her group helped other Ojibwe women, including nineteen girls who arrived directly from the Flandreau boarding school during Jourdain's first months in the city—find jobs and a foothold in their new home. Finding work was difficult for young women without job skills. Jourdain recalled how she landed her first job, with Custom Laundry:

> I sent eight letters. I told them I was a widow with a small child and I had no skills but would volunteer to work free for two weeks until I learned the job. I got five answers, and I took the closest one to save carfare. After all, wages weren't much in those days, just $12 a week.[6]

As the urban Indian community formed, young women found the transition to city life easier when they arrived with friends from the reservation. Amelia Jones, a young job seeker in Minneapolis, shared her story of arriving in 1943, which was the first time she had left her home in Redby, on the Red Lake Reservation. Not quite a high school graduate, she was seventeen. Jones and four of her friends, all Redby girls, left home together for Minneapolis. Like most Ojibwe women who ventured out in the 1940s, they had few resources but were determined and hardworking.

Rural-to-urban migrations for the poor almost always involve working en route to the final destination. Jones and her girlfriends were no exceptions, first stopping to top onions at a farm, then working in a chicken factory in Wells, Minnesota, before landing in Minneapolis. Arriving with no money or savings, they "went to work right away," cleaning houses by the day, getting paid every evening. The young women learned of an employment office and found work cleaning rooms downtown at the Hampshire Arms Hotel, where they lived in a basement annex with "lots of Indians." The experience both terrified and thrilled them; they were teenagers, with no children or husbands, and they felt liberated by the city. Jones recalled their tentative explorations into Minneapolis with humor, remembering that "we were having a big adventure; we were scared to go out at night. We just stayed home, but we managed. . . . We rode the trolley cars to get around town."[7]

After living in the city for a time, the girls went their separate ways. Jones completed high school in Minneapolis, then spent eight months in a vocational school cooking program before becoming a cook in the city for the next thirty-five years. She married Leech Lake Ojibwe Leo Fairbanks in the 1950s, and though they met in Minneapolis, she "first saw him driving a fish truck in Red Lake." Jones was typical of many Ojibwe women who spent their adult working lives in the city: the bonds to her Ojibwe family at Red Lake never diminished, and her apartment became a base for countless relatives who stopped in Minneapolis for shopping trips or to visit sick family members in urban hospitals. She continued to speak Ojibwe with her mother, brothers, and sisters on regular trips to Red Lake. As Jones described her years of urban life, "I always came home. We were always home on the Fourth of July," the time of the annual pow-wow, and like many of her generation, she returned to Red Lake after retirement.[8]

One of Jones' contemporaries among the early community of urban Ojibwe people was Ignatia Broker, who arrived in the city during the year of the attack on Pearl Harbor, and who later wrote an intergenerational memoir of the women in her family, *Night Flying Woman*. Broker was twenty-two when she began attending night classes and worked in a defense plant; later she wrote about the war years as "unstable for everyone, and more so for the Indian people." She lived in a tiny, congested room with six other people during the war, sleeping on small cots in shifts. Still, they opened their door to other Ojibwe who needed a hand.

Though Ojibwe women found jobs in the city, they became part of a decades-long struggle for human rights and equality in employment, housing, education, and social welfare. Broker and her community experienced racial discrimination on a wide array of fronts.[9] She described its impact on the Minneapolis–St. Paul Indian community:

Although employment was good because of the labor demand of the huge defense plants, Indian people faced discrimination in restaurants, night clubs, retail and department stores, in service organizations, public offices, and worst of all, in housing. I can remember hearing, "This room has been rented already, but I got a basement that has a room. I'll show you." I looked at the room. It had the usual rectangular window, and pipes ran overhead. The walls and floors were brown cement, but the man with a gift-giving tone in his voice said, "I'll put linoleum on the floor for you and you'll have a toilet all to yourself. You could wash at the laundry tubs." There was, of course, nothing listed with the War Price and Rationing Board, but the man said it would cost seven dollars a week. I know that he would have made the illegal offer only to an Indian because he knew of the desperate housing conditions we, the first Americans, faced.[10]

Many of the Ojibwe women who joined the migration to urban areas had failed to find jobs in reservation border towns. These towns capitalized on the presence of the Ojibwe by luring tourists to the north woods with picturesque imagery, but they also locked Indian participants out of the local economy, except as performers and consumers. Bemidji, Minnesota, was thirty miles from the borders of the Red Lake Reservation and a shorter distance from Leech Lake, and was the central shopping destination for hundreds of Ojibwe by mid-century. Roberta Head McKenzie of the Red Lake Reservation remembered, "Oh yes, Bemidji didn't like us," even at a time when her two brothers were risking their lives in the military during World War Two. Her father, Selam Head, worked as a lumber grader at the reservation sawmill and toiled for long hours six days a week during the war. McKenzie, small as a child and later a petite adult, was a favorite of an aunt and uncle who had no children, and they helped her attend school in Oklahoma for a time before she returned to Red Lake in 1947 to graduate from high school. After the war, in 1950, McKenzie became a mother while attending a vocational program for secretarial training in Bemidji. Upon finishing her courses, she painfully discovered that the border town was entirely closed to Indians seeking jobs. She began working Saturdays as a file clerk for a small ice cream business in town, but when the owner came into the office and discovered a young Ojibwe woman, McKenzie remembered, "he was really outraged" and "didn't want me out in front in the office." She lost even her meager part-time job.[11]

Without hope of finding work closer to home in Bemidji, McKenzie was accepted into the relocation program in the early 1950s through the Bureau of Indian Affairs area office in Minneapolis; she then spent most of the decade working as a medical secretary at the University of Minnesota. Nationally, the rural-to-urban migration gathered momentum when, in 1952, relocation expanded from the Southwest to more cities, including Cleveland, Dallas, Oklahoma City, Tulsa, San Francisco, and Minneapolis. The relocation program, conceived as the twin to termination, was also part of the federal plan to sever the government's responsibilities to tribal nations in the postwar years. Relocation offered American Indians over the age of eighteen a hand in seeking urban employment, a bus or train ticket, and sometimes basic toiletries and domestic goods, including the ubiquitous alarm clock, once they arrived. McKenzie recalled those first weeks in Minneapolis.

We went to see the BIA agent and he gave us money to ride the bus. They had streetcars then. We looked around for apartments. And as soon as we found one we notified him and he went there and got some money to pay our rent until we got paid. They would pay our rent and give us food. But see, I had to go a whole month, because the state just paid every two weeks on the 15th and 1st. [12]

The BIA relocation program covered apartment rental expenses for the first month in Minneapolis and other designated relocation cities. McKenzie moved into an efficiency apartment with Doris Graves Carlson, a friend from Red Lake who had also attended business school. The program has been sharply criticized for abandoning American Indians who continued to need services and assistance in the city, but McKenzie was prepared for employment and happy for the opportunity to come to Minneapolis and earn a living to support her young family. She had good memories of her relocation, which was not always the case for American Indians, but it is no small point that the Ojibwe found jobs in the city that had been unavailable to them in reservation border towns. Like many relocated Ojibwe people, however, McKenzie conceived of Red Lake as her true community, and she returned in 1958.[13]

A generation of Ojibwe women stayed in Minneapolis to attend school, seek employment, and raise families. Their efforts and connections were essential to the development of a complex of organizations and networks that formed the bedrock of the urban Indian community. Already tested by growing up on reservations during the war or living in boarding schools, they brought their hard-won knowledge to urban life and forged new communities. Gertrude Howard Buckanaga's childhood, spent near Ponsford, on the White Earth Reservation, during a time of family rice camps and blueberry picking, was tragically interrupted in 1946 after her mother, Sadie Howard, died in a car accident, leaving behind seven children. In the aftermath, Buckanaga and five brothers and sisters left for Pipestone, one of the Indian boarding schools still operating in the Midwest. Family remained an important part of her life; the children saw one another at meals and on the playground, and their father regularly visited them at school. She first arrived in Minneapolis during the summer of 1952 as a teenager, working as a nanny to a nine-year-old girl, the daughter of a wealthy lawyer. Buckanaga remembered fixing the girl's meals and taking her to the park, while the little girl introduced her to the library and served as a summer guide, teaching her about the city. After graduating from Pipestone the following year, Buckanaga moved to Minneapolis permanently, at a time when "the Indian community wasn't as big" as today and most people lived near Elliot Park, near the city's downtown.[14]

From the earliest days of the nascent Indian community in Minneapolis, women quickly grew into significant positions of leadership and directed their efforts and labor toward the well-being of children and families. In the process, they created distinctive patterns of white-collar labor around education and social and child welfare. Ojibwe women, including Emily Peake, Gertrude Howard Buckanaga, Frances Fairbanks, Ona Kingbird, Norby Blake, Pat Bellanger, and many others, laid a foundation for new institutions and laws that have been extraordinarily influential and long-lived, not only in Minneapolis but across the United States. They were also adept at influencing a younger, college-educated cohort of Ojibwe women, including Rose Robinson and Vikki Howard, to follow in their footsteps in the community.

Over time, the community grew more focused. Buckanaga recalled the moment in the late 1950s and early 1960s when Indian people began to organize for change in Minneapolis. Informal networks, the ball games and baby showers, were early channels for socialization that led to more lasting efforts in improving community life and social services. A significant moment was the incorporation of the Upper Midwest American Indian Center, in 1961. Buckanaga spoke about the early days:

> They used to do a lot of fundraising, grass roots fundraising like raffles and stuff like that, to help other people who were moving into the urban area. I remember when they incorporated

because we used to come to all those meetings way back. They were different Indian people at that time that were kind of shakers and movers. I learned a lot from them because they were here and they were helping people move into the urban community. Because I remember people didn't realize how racist it was. It was really bad before 1964. [15]

Buckanaga herself led a sit-in at Concordia College in St. Paul, where she had enrolled, intent on earning an elementary school teaching degree. A mother with children in public school, she had grown exasperated with prejudice and the failure of private and public schools in the Twin Cities to meet the needs of Indian children. She became friends with African-American students and joined forces with them to confront the administration regarding the disproportionate amount of money that went to scholarships for white students. While the public perception was that minorities had a free ride in school, Buckanaga knew the reality from her part-time job in the college's financial aid office: few scholarships went to minorities. Her concern for the welfare of Indian children led to a lifelong career in education and social work in the St. Paul and Minneapolis public schools. She eventually helped draft the tribal community college bill. Buckanaga gained her license in social work and continued to assist the Indian community, especially by overseeing an extensive array of services to low-income tribal people in Hennepin County starting in 1986, when she became the executive director of the Upper Midwest American Indian Center.

Contemporary activists on adoption issues refer back to the 1940s, the time directly following the boarding school period, as the beginning of the "adoption era" for American Indian children in the United States.[16] Reservation hardships and urban poverty had placed a large burden on families; the largely white employees of social service agencies sought solutions to complex problems, including mental illness, alcoholism, and family violence, by removing children not only from the troubled parents but from the Indian community—permanently. It has been estimated that perhaps 25 percent of White Earth children left the reservation for foster and adoptive homes in the postwar years.[17] Red Lake and White Earth had the highest rates of child removal within the state of Minnesota, and at the height of the crisis, the "ratio of Indian to non-Indian children in placement was five to one," while in Wisconsin, "Indian children were placed in either foster care or adoptive homes at a rate of 15 to 17 times higher than other children."[18]

During subsequent decades, reservation enrollment offices and staff often felt helpless as Ojibwe adults from across the United States wrote to and phoned councils requesting information about their families, desperate to locate loved ones and understand their own tribal identity. Sandra White Hawk, a Lakota activist and national expert on adoption, credits women in the urban community of Minneapolis–St. Paul for paving the way for the Indian Child Welfare Act (ICWA) of 1978. Women like White Earth tribal member Norby Blake and Peggy Matler, who worked in child welfare during the 1970s, gathered testimony that was used to develop the legislation, though Sen. James Abourezk of South Dakota introduced the act to the Senate Committee on Indian Affairs and is often given credit for the bill. The ICWA was an important recognition of sovereignty in the self-determination era and protected the interests of Indian families and tribal nations "to establish standards for placement of Indian children in foster or adoptive homes, to prevent the break-up of Indian families," while promoting tribal jurisdiction over child custody proceedings.[19]

Rose Robinson was a teacher on the Leech Lake Reservation at the time of the passage of the Indian Child Welfare Act, but soon she began working for the Minnesota Chippewa Tribe as a social services program developer. Robinson reminds people that the ICWA was an "unfunded mandate" that left administrators with few means to achieve its goals. In response, she went to local counties in northern Minnesota to request financial support and entered into negotiations with the state to meet the requirements of the new law. Robinson recalled a difficult time when she had to quit working for the Leech Lake Band in the 1980s, discouraged over political issues and feeling that progress was stalled. She also believed that the team of women working for the tribe who were writing and receiving the grants were not respected or recognized for their hard work, as women should be by their Ojibwe colleagues. It helped Robinson to remember her father's experience working for the tribe and traveling to Washington a generation earlier, and how he had sought out the best possible source for advice, which was his own elderly mother. Robinson drew strength from the example of her father's reliance on his mother and on the historical "position of respect" for female elders.

> Before he went to Washington, DC, that time, he went and sat with my grandma for hours before he went. She spoke Ojibwe. I don't know what they talked about but he made sure he went to talk with her before he went. She was very sharp and she knew how things should be. She wasn't mean to anybody but her husband [laughter]. She was not mean. She was very firm. She'd say you can't be doing that. In Ojibwe. Tell the kids no, no, no. They'd all be scared of her. But she was trying to teach us. We have those old ways that we should really learn from. I think if we did that we'd be a stronger community.[20]

Robinson left northern Minnesota to work in the Minneapolis community for the Minnesota Indian Women's Resource Center. Founded in 1984 to empower women and their families by promoting good health through a comprehensive range of social services, the center was located in the Phillips neighborhood of Minneapolis, by then the third-largest urban Indian community in the country. There, Robinson enjoyed the mentorship of the center's founding director, Cherokee social worker Margaret Peake Raymond. With a growing résumé of child welfare experience, Robinson took a position as specialist in the field with Minnesota's Department of Human Services and worked toward her master's degree in social work at the University of Minnesota. She eventually returned to Leech Lake to be the director of the child welfare program but acknowledged that the work of a child welfare agency is hard, especially as babies are "born positive with drugs in their system," and even harder because one is "related to half the rez." Still, Robinson regards her long career in child welfare as "my life's work" as an Ojibwe woman, and she appreciates the importance of passing on to other women the skills necessary to stand up against the state and county bureaucracies, in a configuration where "the system works against the tribes."

> We had a staff meeting today and I said, "You're all doing a great job." This is what we're here for. This is the tribe taking over this work. It's not the county saying to the community you've got to do it this way. It's the tribe. We're involved. It's about self-determination.[21]

Ojibwe women became leaders in Minneapolis and sustained community life in the city and on reservations through their activism and family advocacy. Incredibly, they achieved college degrees while raising children as they simultaneously pursued meaningful jobs, cared for parents and other family members, and mentored other women. Rose Robinson remembered the dedication of Gertrude Buckanaga of the Upper Midwest American Indian Center; Frances Fairbanks, founding director of the Minneapolis American Indian Center; and others in Minneapolis during the 1960s and 1970s who each had "this passion to help our communities."[22]

When a new Minneapolis American Indian Center opened in 1975 in the Phillips neighborhood, the heart of the urban community, it became a distinctive hub of urban life and social services for an American Indian population that may have exceeded fourteen thousand in both Minneapolis and St. Paul. In the 1970s, the architecturally modern center, with its beautiful wood collage designed by Ojibwe artist George Morrison, was a bright spot on Franklin Avenue, a neighborhood otherwise notorious for urban blight and lively Indian bars. Because the postwar years and the experience of termination were so inextricably linked to poverty, substandard housing, discrimination in education, and a lack of basic services to Indians in the city, these circumstances profoundly influenced the decisions of many Ojibwe women to pursue careers in social welfare to meet the needs of their community. The Minneapolis American Indian Center immediately became a hub of education and social service activity, one that employed many women.

Ignatia Broker, whose husband died during the Korean War, recalled a time when "no Indian family dared approach the relief and welfare agencies of the Twin Cities. They knew that they would only be given a bus ticket and be told to go back to the reservation where the government would take care of them as usual."[23] Women's activities in developing intertribal organizations and founding Indian centers like those in Minneapolis and Chicago can all be traced to the long list of deficiencies in urban Indian life in the postwar and termination era cities of the Great Lakes region.[24]

Ojibwe people did not completely escape either poverty or discrimination in the city and were increasingly concerned about police violence toward American Indians in the 1960s and 1970s. Significantly, they also lacked health care and some of the other benefits of residing on the reservation. When a group began meeting in the summer of 1968 to address and challenge the problems urban Indians faced—"prisons, courts, police, treaties, the government," in the words of Dennis Banks—Ojibwe women were part of every forum. Banks recalled that at an early meeting, when the group still had no formal name, "a woman stood up and said, 'You always aim to do this and to do that. Why don't we just call ourselves AIM?'"[25] The organization that emerged from that community forum, the American Indian Movement, made Minneapolis into a national center of Indian activism for the next decade.

In 1968, AIM was one of many similar organizations that had emerged in urban areas throughout the United States and Canada with sizable American Indian populations. AIM's home base was Minneapolis, but soon chapters were organized in cities such as Milwaukee and Cleveland, and over the next few years the group grew into a stronger national organization. During its early days, members directly challenged law enforcement and civil authorities by setting up the AIM Patrol to help combat the problem of police brutality and racism. AIM found high visibility and success in its early years, a time that included momentous episodes, such as the takeover of both Alcatraz Island, near San Francisco, and the Bureau of Indian Affairs building in Washington, D.C., as well as the 1973 events surrounding Wounded Knee. The group's leaders, especially founders Dennis Banks, Clyde Bellecourt, Eddie Benton-Benai, and George Mitchell, were well-known for their successful use of symbols and the media to publicize problems faced by American Indians in urban areas. Their efforts raised the

American consciousness about the historic mistreatment of the indigenous people of the United States and Canada. AIM is acknowledged for the pride it created in American Indians, especially a generation of urban youth, at a time when people were still coping with the postwar policies of termination and relocation.[26]

Though the conventional narrative of AIM tends to focus on its male founders and early successes, a history of the movement more attentive to the issue of gender produces a very different narrative. Indeed, women's efforts have been overshadowed by the presence of highly charismatic men, and the rich and significant involvement of these women in AIM has been somewhat hidden in the history of Indian activism. Journalistic reports of that involvement have tended to focus on the lone female figure of Anna Mae Aquash, the Mi'kmaq activist who was murdered during the winter of 1976, yet many women played developmental roles in the movement from the outset. Their work in the early years laid a foundation for new institutions for education and social welfare that have been extraordinarily long-lived in the Indian community.

Women turned their attention to publicizing and solving problems on a wide range of social issues. Leech Lake Ojibwe Pat Bellanger and many other women attended the early Minneapolis forums organized in the summer of 1968. Once again, child welfare emerged as a significant area of work for AIM women because of pleas from parents whose children were being removed, and Bellanger received countless phone calls from members of the community families. She recalled that in the Twin Cities, Ramsey and Hennepin Counties "were taking Indian children from homes where they felt that the child wasn't being educated, that they were being made a failure, and so they were put into white homes. And so the parents were panicking, saying, 'My child is good, I have a good kid,' yet Indians were not succeeding in mainstream public schools."[27]

Vikki Howard was a Leech Lake teenager living in Minneapolis when she first learned about the American Indian Movement. During the takeover of Alcatraz, she and her public school classmates at North High School, who affiliated with AIM youth and called themselves TANS, for True American Native Students, coordinated a tour of "all the Indian boarding schools from Minnesota to southern California, to Alcatraz and back." They reached Alcatraz toward the end of the occupation, and Howard returned to the Twin Cities to enter Macalester College, in St. Paul, during the year of Wounded Knee, the highly symbolic AIM takeover on the Pine Ridge Reservation, in South Dakota, in 1973, which focused national attention on Indian issues. Some of Howard's friends went out to South Dakota while she "stayed focused" in college. The later trials at the federal building in St. Paul, during which AIM leaders were acquitted of wrongdoing during the takeover, and the formation of new, alternative "survival" schools in the Twin Cities, where part of the activist agenda would be fulfilled through the establishment of an indigenous-focused curriculum, left Howard feeling that there was "never a dull moment."[28] She recalled the event known as the Longest Walk, the 1978 journey from San Francisco to Washington, D.C., organized by activists to create greater awareness across the country of American Indian concerns.

As I grew into a young adult, in my twenties with the American Indian Movement, I went on the Longest Walk in 1978. . . . I ended up going out with the Minnesota team, the group that went from Minnesota AIM. The original AIM. Quite a few people from the community. I got to do work on some of the logistics and public relations, and designing pamphlets to educate people why the Longest Walk was happening. Through the movement I was exposed to my first Sun

Dance and spirituality, different elders. All this came about
as I started working at Heart of the Earth. And that's when
I began my journey to find my way and that's where I found
my way back to the Anishinaabe way of life.[29]

Howard spent ten years after college working at the Heart of
the Earth Survival School in Minneapolis, innovating for her students in the seventh through twelfth grades curriculum in history
and social studies in ways that included American Indian history
and culture. She eventually became the elementary school's principal. Heart of the Earth was one of two American Indian Movement
survival schools formed in the Twin Cities in 1972. The other was
the Red School House, in St. Paul, which closed in 1995 while
Heart of the Earth continued until 2008. Ona Kingbird, Pat Bellanger, Vikki Howard, and many other Ojibwe women committed
their skills, creativity, labor, and leadership to the education of
urban Indian children through the survival schools, which outlived
by many years the early symbolic and well-known AIM protests of
the 1970s. The women's decades-long work to create culturally and
historically meaningful curricula outlasted the survival schools
themselves and influenced a new generation of charter schools,
language-immersion schools, and more mainstream institutions
throughout Minnesota. Remembering her own coming-of-age with
the American Indian Movement, Howard reflected, "It was a good
time in history to be growing up in the Twin Cities American
Indian community; it was like the renaissance of American Indian
everything."[30]

The generations born after the allotment of reservations, assimilation, and subsequent disruptive policies of the termination era
were left to pick up the pieces, and they did not forget the experiences of their parents and grandparents. While many stayed in the

Ojibwe homelands on reservations, others migrated to the cities of the Great Lakes region and forged a new pan-indigenous community in the urban landscape. Remarkably, Ojibwe culture and ethics of community life persisted in the aftermath of greater urbanization and still thrive in unexpected ways in cities like Minneapolis. Ignatia Broker, the World War Two defense worker and later a storyteller and author, described hardship but also fortitude, generosity, and a new kinship that crossed tribal lines, resulting in the distinctive urban Indian community that emerged in Minneapolis and other cities in the twentieth century.

> Maybe it was a good thing, the migration of our people to the urban areas during the war years, because there, amongst the millions of people, we were brought to a brotherhood. We Indian people who worked in the war plants started a social group not only for the Ojibway but for the Dakota, the Arikara, the Menominee, the Gros Ventres, the Cree, the Oneida, and all those from other tribes and other states who had made the trek to something new.[31]

Scholars writing about the twentieth-century struggles of Indian people for greater tribal sovereignty have emphasized the historic nineteen-month takeover of Alcatraz that began on November 20, 1969, as a beginning benchmark for activism, yet Indian leaders and foundational organizations had certainly undertaken formative political efforts in the early postwar years through the 1960s and beyond. In taking this longer and broader view of Indian activism, the definition of meaningful action expands to include a variety of significant responsibilities through which people behaved in "politically purposeful ways." Usually this means reconsidering the more mundane aspects of organized political action, like arranging community meetings, writing grants, coordinating youth programs, and testifying before local and state political bodies, in addition to militancy.[32]

Ojibwe women worked alongside men, within their communities, to take control of their own destinies. The women themselves remain outspoken yet humble and are likely to cite male leaders in the community for their ability to give good speeches or create political change. However, in the long view of the history of American Indian activism in Minneapolis, it is clear that women held the majority of sustained leadership roles in the community through their participation in the less sensational but no less important or visionary work of organizing new schools, Indian centers, curricula, social services, and legislation. Their body of work, especially new varieties of white-collar labor, is a breathtaking achievement that led to increased well-being for Indians in Minnesota and greater sovereignty for Indian people nationwide.[33]

Ojibwe women's underlying commitment to values they learned from their mothers, grandmothers, and other significant figures in their lives remains a powerful influence. They are keenly aware of having inherited a responsibility from previous generations who weathered great hardships. Pat Bellanger expressed admiration for how boldly Ojibwe women "have been strong throughout everything" and insisted that "we have kept our ways." Women including Bellanger have an appreciation for the historical role of women in Ojibwe society and the fact that some of the most important work that sustained community life, like harvesting wild rice, "has always gone through the women."[34] Like their Ojibwe grandmothers, they continue to work as women did in the wild rice economy—not only for material sustenance but for their own empowerment and the spiritual well-being of their family and community.

ACKNOWLEDGMENTS

☯

Aaniin! I wish to express my gratitude to many wonderful colleagues, students, friends, and family members who live and work in Ojibwe Country. The fine people who make up the departments of American Studies, American Indian Studies, and History at the University of Minnesota have challenged me to think deeply and critically about issues of gender and American Indian history, and I appreciate their encouragement and fellowship. It is a privilege for me to work surrounded by scholars who have shaped conversations in my field, and to be part of the vibrant and remarkable Indian community of Minneapolis and St. Paul.

For their generous support while researching this book, I am deeply grateful to the staff of the Minnesota Historical Society. They have not only provided me with a fantastic hideaway—an office just steps from the library and archives for writing—but many librarians, curators, and other staff who work at this significant institution have been generous with their time and support for my projects, including this book. Erik Redix, Karissa White, and Kasey Keeler were essential research assistants, and I thank them for the long hours they logged on my behalf not only at the Minnesota Historical Society and University Libraries, but in Erik's case also in the National Archives. Karissa was invaluable for oral histories conducted in Minneapolis and northern Minnesota. I must also thank Kevin Doughten, my thoughtful editor, and members of the advisory board for the Penguin Library of American Indian History who, along with Carolyn Carlson, suggested there be a book about the Ojibwe in this series.

I am deeply grateful for the intellectual fellowship and friendship of many Ojibwe writers and scholars, and have learned so much from Kim Blaeser, John Borrows, Louise Erdrich, Anton Treuer, Gerald Vizenor, Michael Witgen, and others in the strong circles who write about the Ojibwe people. I am also grateful to my colleague John Nichols, who advised me about Ojibwe words and spellings in the book, and gave me positive advice and encouragement. I have great admiration for the work and spirit of the Ojibwe women interviewed for the Ojibwe Women Oral History Project. Their ideas and words allowed me to write a chapter about the Minneapolis American Indian community.

My son, Frankie, likes to refer to the annual meetings of the American Society for Ethnohistory as "Ethnohistory Camp," and I admit that members of this congenial group of scholars take unusual pleasure in our yearly get-togethers. For their endurance and commitment to getting it right while having fun I am thankful for David Edmunds, Rayna Green, John Troutman, Brian Klopotek, Jeffrey Ostler, Jenny Tone-Pa-Hote, Keith Richotte, Heidi Stark, Jill Doerfler, Chantal Norrgard, Kate Williams, Erik Redix, Jean O'Brien, Patrick McNamara, Pat Albers, Bruce White, Jacqueline Peterson, Susan Sleeper-Smith, Jacki Rand, Raymond Fogelson, Tsianina Lomawaima, Colin Calloway, Frederick Hoxie, and all the ethnohistorians I enjoy meeting up with in a new location every year, from Quebec City to Mexico City. Our wonderful colleague, Helen H. Tanner, would have enjoyed seeing this book in print.

This book about Ojibwe women, along with my earlier *Boarding School Seasons*, both found inspiration in the strength of Ojibwe family and community life. The extended families named Auginash, Child, and McNamara all inspire me in their own ways. To say they are merely supportive of my work is an underestimation of their gifts to me, but with Pat, Frankie, Benay, and Uncle Brian at the center of my life, I am reminded of my good fortune. Miigwech!

NOTES

⊛

INTRODUCTION: *Maps of Birch Bark*

1. The first Ojibwe written account of the migration occurs in William W. Warren, *History of the Ojibwe People* (St. Paul: Minnesota Historical Society Press, 1984; originally published 1885).
2. For all Ojibwe spellings I have referred to John D. Nichols and Earl Nyholm, *A Concise Dictionary of Minnesota Ojibwe* (Minneapolis: University of Minnesota Press, 1995). I have also consulted with my colleague Professor Nichols about Ojibwe spellings and words used in the book. Ojibwe words in this book are written in the modern writing system for Ojibwe, except those taken from historical sources, where they are written as they appear in the source. In these cases, the modern spelling and possible meaning is noted after first use.
3. Richard White, *The Middle Ground: Indians, Empires, and Republics in the Great Lakes Region, 1650–1815* (Cambridge: Cambridge University Press, 1991).
4. Michael Witgen, *An Infinity of Nations: How the Native World Shaped Modern North America* (Philadelphia: University of Pennsylvania Press, 2011).
5. The essential source for historical maps of Indian Country in the Great Lakes is Helen Hornbeck Tanner, *Atlas of Great Lakes Indian History* (Norman: University of Oklahoma Press, 1987).
6. Charles A. Eastman, *Indian Heroes and Great Chieftains* (Mineola, N.Y.: Dover, 1997; originally published 1918): 226–27.
7. Douglas Leighton, "The Manitoulin Incident of 1863: An Indian-White Confrontation," *Ontario History* 69:2 (June 1977): 113–24.
8. The Sandy Lake Tragedy is discussed in chapter 3. On Sandy Lake, see James Clifton, "Wisconsin Death March: Explaining the Extremes in Old Northwest Indian Removal," *Transactions of the Wisconsin Academy of Sciences, Arts and Letters* 75 (1987): 1–39; Ronald N. Satz, "The Removal Order and the Wisconsin Death March," in *Chippewa Treaty Rights: The Reserved Rights of Wisconsin's Chippewa Indians in Historical Perspective,*

Transactions of the Wisconsin Academy of Sciences, Arts and Letters 79, no. 1 (1991): 51–59; and Bruce White, "The Regional Context of the Removal Order of 1850," in *Fish in the Lakes, Wild Rice, and Game in Abundance: Testimony on Behalf of Mille Lacs Ojibwe Hunting and Fishing Rights*, ed. James M. McClurken (East Lansing: Michigan State University Press, 2000), 141–328.

9. William W. Warren, *History of the Ojibwe People* (St. Paul: Minnesota Historical Society Press, 1984; originally published 1885).

10. See James W. Oberly, "Land, Population, Prices, and the Regulation of Natural Resources: The Lake Superior Ojibwa, 1790–1920," in *The Other Side of the Frontier: Economic Explorations into Native American History*, ed. Linda Barrington (Boulder, CO: Westview Press, 1999); and Russell Thornton, "Health, Disease, and Demography," in *A Companion to American Indian History*, eds. Philip J. Deloria and Neal Salisbury (Malden, MA: Blackwell Publishers, 2002), 68–84.

11. Land cessions in the United States were generally calculated in acres. In 1837, the Lake Superior Ojibwe ceded 14 million acres.

12. U.S. Census Bureau, 2002; Indian and Northern Affairs Canada, 2004.

13. Kevin K. Washburn, "The Legacy of *Bryan v. Itasca County:* How a $147 County Tax Notice Helped Bring Tribes $200 Billion in Indian Gaming Revenue," *Minnesota Law Review* 92, no. 4 (April 2008): 919–70.

14. Brenda J. Child, *Boarding School Seasons: American Indian Families, 1900–1940* (Lincoln: University of Nebraska Press, 1998).

15. The name Nodinens is from *noodinens*, "little wind."

1. WOMEN OF THE GREAT LAKES AND MISSISSIPPI:
Everything Was Very Systematic

1. The Mississippi River first flows north to Lake Bemidji before heading east and south, a fact that confused early European settlers and explorers.

2. Henry Schoolcraft may have been the first to call it Lake Itasca, but he acknowledged that the Ojibwe referred to the lake as "Omushkos," which means "elk."

3. Ojibwe names found in historical accounts ranged from formal names that came from visions and ceremonies to very informal nicknames. Ne Zet is probably a nickname, possibly *nizid*, "my foot."

4. Bellanger and Carl were members of an early intertribal organization in Minneapolis and St. Paul, the Ojibway-Dakota Research Society. This story was written down and is in the collections of the Papers of Emily Peake, Research File on Minnesota Ojibwe Women, Minnesota Historical Society.

5. A long body of anthropological literature on coming-of-age among indigenous peoples exists. One study that has examined indigenous practices with an emphasis on female rituals is Carol A. Markstrom, *Empowerment of North American Indian Girls: Ritual Expressions at Puberty* (Lincoln: University of Nebraska Press, 2008).

6. Bellanger and Carl, 3, Papers of Emily Peake.

7. Henry Schoolcraft, *The Indian Tribes of the United States, Volume 1* (Philadelphia: Lippincott, Grambo, and Co., 1851), 209–10.

8. Frances Densmore, *Chippewa Customs* (St. Paul: Minnesota Historical Society Press, 1979; originally published 1929), 60.

9. *Doodem* is a word stem that cannot stand alone in Ojibwe conversation but must have a prefix indicating the possessor. For example, *indoodem* is "my clan," *gidoodem* is "your clan."

10. This idea is suggested in a number of works about the Ojibwe, including Basil Johnston, *Ojibway Heritage* (Toronto: McCleland & Stewart, 1976), 119–33.

11. Henry Rowe Schoolcraft referred to Wabose as the "Prophetess of Chegoimegon" in a lengthy discussion of her life and songs and she drew the story of her vision. Her drawings were later transferred into a drawing by Seth Eastman, "Vision of Catherine Wabose," *The Indian Tribes of the United States*, Volume I, 388-401.

12. Ibid., 388-401.

13. A number of scholars have weighed in on Ojibwe women and puberty traditions since the early work of Schoolcraft. They include Inez M. Hilger, *Chippewa Child Life and Its Cultural Background* (St. Paul: Minnesota Historical Society Press, 1992; originally published 1951); Densmore, *Chippewa Customs*; Johnston, *Ojibway Heritage*; Vine Deloria, Jr., *The World We Used to Live In: Remembering the Powers of the Medicine Man* (Golden, CO: Fulcrum Publishing, 2006); and Markstrom, *Empowerment of North American Indian Girls*.

14. Densmore, *Chippewa Customs*, 61.

15. Federal Writers' Project of the Works Progress Administration, *The WPA Guide to Wisconsin* (St. Paul: Minnesota Historical Society Press, 2006; originally published 1941), 38.

16. While scholars classify Ojibwe people as patrilineal and patrilocal, Densmore (*Chippewa Customs*, 60) found that Ojibwe households in early-twentieth-century Minnesota generally had "one or more grandparents" and that "a man usually lived with his wife's family, hence the old people were her parents."

17. Anton Treuer, *The Assassination of Hole in the Day* (St. Paul: Minnesota Historical Society Press, 2010).

18. Charles A. Eastman, *Indian Heroes and Great Chieftains* (Mineola, N.Y.: Dover, 1997; originally published 1918), 233.

19. Ibid., 227.
20. Julia Warren Spears, "Reminiscences of a Short History of the Chippewa Chief Hole in the Day . . . ," Julia A. Spears and Family Papers, 1839–1923, Minnesota Historical Society.
21. Eastman, *Indian Heroes and Great Chieftains*.
22. Spears, "Reminiscences."
23. Quikabanokwe is possibly Gwekaabanookwe, "turning dawn woman."
24. Minisinokwog is Minisinaakwaang, an unknown location in Wisconsin. The meaning may be idiomatic.
25. Gotchijigijig is spelled Gojijiigiizhig in modern usage. Pakwewang is a common landscape description in Ojibwe, and numerous locations in northern Wisconsin and Minnesota have this name or some variant. For example, two Lac Courte Oreilles communities in the nineteenth century were called this: one on the Chippewa River that was within the reservation boundary and another on the Namekagon River near Seeley, Wisconsin. The word's modern spelling is Bakweyawaa, which refers to an inlet or a bay in a river.
26. Jerome Arbuckle, "Qui-ka-ba-no-kwe—'Dawn Woman,' " Works Progress Administration, Chippewa Indian Historical Project Records, Archives of the Franciscan Sisters of Perpetual Adoration, La Crosse, Wisconsin, Envelope 12, 32. This underutilized WPA project, based on the Bad River Reservation under the direction of Sister Macaria Murphy, contains valuable information on a variety of topics related to Ojibwe history in Wisconsin and Upper Michigan. The original records were later shipped back to Sister Murphy's convent in La Crosse, where they remain; the State Historical Society of Wisconsin also microfilmed the records, which are available at the Area Research Center in Ashland, Wisconsin.
27. Ibid., 34.
28. Ibid.
29. Ibid.
30. Frances Densmore, *Strength of the Earth: The Classic Guide to Ojibwe Uses of Native Plants* (St. Paul: Minnesota Historical Society Press, 2005; originally published 1928).
31. Richard Erdoes and Alfonso Ortiz relate a version of this story that describes the twins as the offspring of the sun, who impregnated the young woman. One of the twins was Stone Boy, who was a rock, but his brother was Nanabozhoo. *American Indian Myths and Legends* (New York: Pantheon Books, 1984), 150–51.
32. Bruce White, *We Are at Home: Pictures of the Ojibwe People* (St. Paul: Minnesota Historical Society Press, 2007), 20–31.
33. Florina Denomie, Chippewa Indian Historical Project.

34. The dream catcher has become ubiquitous, but it originates with Ojibwe people in the Great Lakes. Densmore (*Chippewa Customs*, 52) described historical dream catchers: "The web was made of nettle-stalk twine and colored dark red with the juice of the bloodroot and the inner bark of the wild plum."

35. Ibid., 61–62.

36. Ibid., 119–23.

37. The collections of the Minnesota Historical Society hold many items of material culture that Densmore collected in the early twentieth century. Other voice recordings and music may be found in the Smithsonian Institution and the Library of Congress.

38. Charles E. Cleland describes how the Ojibwe hunted their way north in *Fish in the Lakes, Wild Rice, and Game in Abundance*, ed. James M. McClurken (East Lansing: Michigan State University Press, 2000).

39. Densmore, *Chippewa Customs*, 122.

40. Ibid.

41. Susan Sleeper-Smith, *Indian Women and French Men: Rethinking Cultural Encounter in the Western Great Lakes* (Amherst: University of Massachusetts, 2001), 83, 96.

42. Arbuckle, "Qui-ka-ba-no-kwe—'Dawn Woman,'" 31–37.

43. Collections of the Minnesota Historical Society, Daniel Stanchfield, *History of Lumbering in Minnesota,* Volume 9, 1901, 331–32.

44. Albert E. Jenks, "The Wild Rice Gatherers of the Upper Lakes: A Study in American Primitive Economics," *Nineteenth Annual Report of the Bureau of American Ethnology* 2 (1897–98): 1013–33; Thomas Vennum, Jr., *Wild Rice and the Ojibway People* (St. Paul: Minnesota Historical Society Press, 1988).

45. John Rogers, *Red World and White: Memories of a Chippewa Boyhood* (Norman: University of Oklahoma Press, 1996; originally published 1957), 26.

46. Frances Densmore's study *Chippewa Customs* was first published in 1929 as Bulletin 86 of the Smithsonian Institution Bureau of American Ethnology. For Nodinens' classic account of the Ojibwe year, see pages 119–23 of the 1979 reprint edition previously mentioned.

47. Other indigenous people in North America tell stories of the Earth Diver, including the Haudenosaunee.

48. One of the best Ojibwe storytellers in print is Basil Johnston, a Canadian scholar from Ontario. It is important to remember that all Ojibwe stories were a legacy of an oral tradition, subject to regional variation and interpretation. This passage is taken from Johnston's eastern Ojibwe version of the creation story in his book *Ojibway Heritage*, 14–15.

49. Johnston (Ibid., 61) says the "evidence is strong that the term 'dodaem' comes from the same root as do 'dodum' and 'dodosh.' 'Dodum' means

to do or fulfill, while 'Dodosh' literally means breast, that from which milk, or food, or sustenance is drawn." He goes on to say that "Dodaem" may mean "that from which I draw my purpose, meaning and being."

50. Ibid.

51. The classic source of information on the history and evolution of the Ojibwe *indoodemag* is the nineteenth-century Ojibwe historian William W. Warren's *History of the Ojibwe People* (St. Paul: Minnesota Historical Society Press, 1984; originally published 1885). A more recent study is Heidi Bohaker, "Nindoodemag: The Significance of Algonquian Kinship Networks in the Eastern Great Lakes Region, 1600–1701," *William and Mary Quarterly* 63, no. 1 (January 2006): 23–52.

2. MADELINE ISLAND: *Ojibwe Women in Fur Trade Society*

1. The literature on the history of the fur trade was greatly enhanced beginning in the late 1970s with the growth of scholarship in women's history. Significant studies include Jacqueline Peterson's "Prelude to Red River: A Social Portrait of the Great Lakes Métis," *Ethnohistory* 25, no. 1 (Winter 1978): 41–67; "The People In Between: Indian-White Marriage and the Genesis of a Métis Society and Culture in the Great Lakes Region 1680–1830" (Ph.D. dissertation, University of Illinois–Chicago, 1980); and, with Jennifer S. H. Brown, *The New Peoples: Being and Becoming Métis in North America* (Winnipeg: University of Manitoba Press, 1985). See also Bruce White, "The Woman Who Married a Beaver: Trade Patterns and Gender Roles in the Ojibwa Fur Trade," *Ethnohistory* 46, no. 1 (Winter 1999): 109–47; Jennifer S. H. Brown, *Strangers in Blood: Fur Trade Company Families in Indian Country* (Vancouver: University of British Columbia Press, 1980); Sylvia Van Kirk, *Many Tender Ties: Women in Fur-Trade Society, 1670–1870* (Norman: University of Oklahoma Press, 1983); and Susan Sleeper-Smith, *Indian Women and French Men: Rethinking Cultural Encounter in the Western Great Lakes* (Amherst: University of Massachusetts, 2001).

2. Richard White's influential ethnohistorical study *The Middle Ground: Indians, Empires, and Republics in the Great Lakes Region, 1650–1815* (Cambridge: Cambridge University Press, 1991) introduced the idea of intercultural accommodation between the French and indigenous peoples as a "middle ground."

3. The cliffs are composed of layered sandstone and have a reddish or crimson color.

4. The island was also referred to in their lifetime by Euro-Americans as Michael's Island.

5. William W. Warren, *History of the Ojibwe People* (St. Paul: Minnesota Historical Society Press, 1984; originally published 1885), 213.

6. George Nelson, *My First Years in the Fur Trade*, eds. Theresa Schenck and Laura Peers (St. Paul: Minnesota Historical Society Press, 2002).

7. William Jones, "Ojibwa Tales from the North Shore of Lake Superior," *The Journal of American Folklore* 29, no. 113 (July–Sept. 1916): 368–91.

8. White, "Woman Who Married a Beaver."

9. Zebulon M. Pike, "Pike's Explorations in Minnesota, 1805–6," *Collections of the Minnesota Historical Society* 1 (1872): 368–416.

10. White, "Woman Who Married a Beaver."

11. Ibid., 125.

12. Nelson, *First Years in the Fur Trade*, 25.

13. Netnokwa is spelled Nednaakwe in modern usage and refers to a geographic feature on the shores of Lake Huron, where she was from.

14. Louise Erdrich, introduction to *The Falcon: A Narrative of the Captivity and Adventures of John Tanner*, by John Tanner (New York: Penguin Books, 1994; originally published 1830), xii.

15. This was a time of epidemics introduced by Europeans.

16. Ibid., 84, 241.

17. Ibid., 52.

18. This and previous quote, ibid., 98.

19. Naganabenazekwa is spelled Niigaanibinesiikwe in modern usage and means Leading Thunderbird (or other large bird).

20. Marie Denomie, "The Life of Neaganabenazekwa (Madeline Cloud)," Works Progress Administration, Chippewa Indian Historical Project Records, Archives of the Franciscan Sisters of Perpetual Adoration, La Crosse, Wisconsin, Envelope 19.

21. Ibid.

22. Peterson, "People In Between," 71, 88.

23. Ozhawguscodaywaquay is spelled Ozhaawashodewikwe. Waubojeeg, or White Fisher, is spelled Waabojiig.

24. Charles E. Cleland, *The Place of the Pike (Gnoozhekaaning): A History of the Bay Mills Indian Community* (Ann Arbor: University of Michigan Press, 2001), 9–19.

25. Maureen Konkle, *Writing Indian Nations: Native Intellectuals and the Politics of Historiography, 1827–1863* (Chapel Hill: University of North Carolina Press, 2004); Robert Dale Parker, *The Sound the Stars Make Rushing Through the Sky: The Writings of Jane Johnston Schoolcraft* (Philadelphia: University of Pennsylvania Press, 2007).

26. Hamilton Nelson Ross, *La Pointe, Village Outpost* (St. Paul: North Central Publishing, 1960), 64–65.

27. This is the view of Brown, *Strangers in Blood*, Chapter 6.

28. Nelson, *First Years in the Fur Trade*, 177–78.
29. The term translates as "after the custom of the country" and refers to the idea that early marriages between indigenous women and European men were without formal church sanction.
30. Brown, *Strangers in Blood*, 150.
31. Van Kirk, *Many Tender Ties,* and Brown, *Strangers in Blood*.
32. Theda Perdue, *Cherokee Women: Gender and Culture Change, 1700–1835* (Lincoln: University of Nebraska Press, 1998).
33. Sleeper-Smith, *Indian Women and French Men*.
34. Ibid., 29.
35. Cleland, *Place of the Pike*, 17–30.
36. However, when the treaty was ratified, the U.S. Senate unilaterally struck out this provision.
37. Cleland, *Place of the Pike*, 17-30.
38. Quoted in Charles E. Cleland, *Fish in the Lakes, Wild Rice, and Game in Abundance*, ed. James M. McClurken (East Lansing: Michigan State University Press, 2000), 29.
39. Treaty with the Chippewa, July 29, 1837, 7 Stat., 536, Article 5.
40. Quoted in Theresa M. Schenck, *All Our Relations: Chippewa Mixed Bloods and the Treaty of 1837* (Madison, WI: Amik Press, 2009).
41. Charles J. Kappler, ed., *Indian Affairs: Laws and Treaties,* Vol. 5 (Washington, DC: Government Printing Office, 1904–41), 147–48.
42. Schenck, *All Our Relations*, 8.
43. Charles E. Cleland, "1842 Treaty of LaPointe," in *Fish in the Lakes*, 36–44.
44. Edmund Jefferson Danziger, *The Chippewas of Lake Superior* (Norman: University of Oklahoma Press, 1979), 80–81.
45. Thomas Vennum, "The Ojibwa Begging Dance," in *Music and Context: Essays for John M. Ward*, ed. Anne Dhu Shapiro (Cambridge: Harvard University Press, 1985), 54–78.
46. Ross, *La Pointe*, 86.
47. Danziger, *The Chippewas of Lake Superior*, 87.
48. Ibid., 90.
49. Ross, *La Pointe*.
50. John O. Holzhueter, *Madeline Island and the Chequamegon Region* (Madison: State Historical Society of Wisconsin Press, 1974), 47.
51. Ronald N. Satz, "The Removal Order and the Wisconsin Death March," in *Chippewa Treaty Rights, Transactions of the Wisconsin Academy of Sciences, Arts and Letters* 79, no. 1 (1991): 51–59.
52. William Whipple Warren was born at La Pointe on Madeline Island in 1825.
53. Peterson, "People In Between," 71, 88.

3. RESERVATIONS: *Holding Our World Together*

1. When speaking English, many Ojibwe people today say "that old lady" when referring to a highly regarded female elder. The Ojibwe historian and language teacher Anton Treuer has spoken of *mindimooyenh* as a more complex term than "old woman," and I rely on his interpretation in this chapter.

2. Julia A. Spears and Family Papers, 1839–1923, Minnesota Historical Society.

3. Henry M. Rice to Alexander Ramsey, December 1, 1849, Alexander Ramsey Papers, Microfilm edition, Minnesota Historical Society, M203, Roll 4.

4. Charles J. Kappler, ed., *Indian Affairs: Laws and Treaties, Vol. 5* (Washington, DC: Government Printing Office, 1904–41), 663.

5. Julia A. Spears and Family Papers.

6. Ibid.

7. Rev. Edward Duffield Neill, *The History of Minnesota: From the Earliest French Explorations to the Present Time* (Minneapolis: Minnesota Historical Company, 1882), 549–51.

8. Bruce White, "The Regional Context of the Removal Order of 1850," in *Fish in the Lakes, Wild Rice, and Game in Abundance*, ed. James M. McClurken (East Lansing: Michigan State University Press, 2000), 194.

9. Ibid., 195.

10. Alexander Ramsey Papers, Roll 5, December 3, 1850.

11. Ibid.

12. For an extended discussion of this see Brenda Child and Erik Redix, "Rethinking the Sandy Lake 'Tragedy': Ethnic Cleansing in Minnesota Territory," paper presented at the American Society for Ethnohistory Conference, Eugene, Oregon, November 12, 2008.

13. See James Clifton, "Wisconsin Death March: Explaining the Extremes in Old Northwest Indian Removal," *Transactions of the Wisconsin Academy of Sciences, Arts and Letters* 75 (1987): 1–39; Ronald N. Satz, "The Removal Order and the Wisconsin Death March," in *Chippewa Treaty Rights: The Reserved Rights of Wisconsin's Chippewa Indians in Historical Perspective, Transactions of the Wisconsin Academy of Sciences, Arts and Letters* 79, no. 1 (1991): 51–59; and White, "Regional Context of the Removal Order."

14. As quoted in White, "Regional Context of the Removal Order," 221.

15. Ibid.

16. Ibid., 228.

17. Ibid., 246.

18. Ibid., 247.

19. Especially known for this was the *Lake Superior News and Mining Journal*, published in Sault Ste. Marie and Marquette.

20. Alexander Ramsey left office in the spring of 1853, and John Watrous was arrested the same year.

21. Minnesota became a state in 1858.

22. These were the words of Kawnondowinwinzo and other headmen in an 1867 petition to the Commissioner of Indian Affairs. Quoted in Charles E. Cleland, "The Treaties of 1863 and 1864," in McClurken, *Fish in the Lakes*, 102.

23. Rebecca Kugel, *To Be the Main Leaders of Our People: A History of Minnesota Ojibwe Politics, 1825–1898* (Lansing: Michigan State University, 1998), 120–23.

24. Erwin F. Mittelholtz, *Historical Review of the Red Lake Indian Reservation: A History of Its People and Progress* (Bemidji, MN: Beltrami County Historical Society, 1957).

25. Minnesota Chippewa Tribe, *White Earth: A History* (Cass Lake: Minnesota Chippewa Tribe, 1989), 37.

26. Brenda J. Child and Karissa E. White, " 'I've Done My Share': Ojibwe People and World War II," *Minnesota History* 61, no. 5 (Spring 2009): 196–207.

27. Ibid.

28. Joan Jensen, *Calling This Place Home: Women on the Wisconsin Frontier, 1850–1925* (St. Paul: Minnesota Historical Society Press, 2006), 64–65.

29. The murder of Joe White and the trial of the game warden and deputy were closely followed in local newspapers, including the *Shell Lake Watchman* and the *Spooner Register*, during 1894 and 1895. See also the State Against S. M. Hicks, State Historical Society of Wisconsin, Ashland Area Research Center, Washburn Series 27: Wisconsin Circuit Court Washburn County, Case Files, 1886–1982, ST 113. Also Erik Redix, "The Murder of Joe White and the Impact of States on Inherent Tribal Sovereignty," paper delivered at the Native American and Indigenous Studies Association Annual Conference, Athens, Georgia, April 10, 2008. A full historical study of the murder of Joe White and the ensuing trial has yet to be written.

30. Maude Kegg, *Portage Lake: Memories of an Ojibwe Childhood*, ed. John D. Nichols (Minneapolis: University of Minnesota Press, 1993).

31. Marie Livingston, "Blueberrying Forty-Five Years Ago—Strange but True," Works Progress Administration: Chippewa Indian Historical Project Records, Archives of the Franciscan Sisters of Perpetual Adoration, La Crosse, Wisconsin, Envelope 8, 31.

32. Florina Denomie, "Picking Blueberries in Northern Wisconsin," Works Progress Administration: Chippewa Indian Historical Project Records, Envelope 8, 29.

33. Nodinens, as you recall, was a Mille Lacs woman who eloquently detailed the Ojibwe seasonal round to Frances Densmore.

34. Ben Gauthier was a tribal member, while his wife was non-Indian. Their Gauthier Hotel opened in 1891 as the first hotel on the reservation; it catered to lumber mill employees and was the predecessor to the resort. Surveys of Indian Industry, 282203, Lac du Flambeau Agency, 1922, National Archives and Records Administration, Records Group 75, Records of the Bureau of Indian Affairs, Great Lakes Region, Chicago, Illinois.

35. Surveys of Indian Industry, 28224.

36. Surveys of Indian Industry, 282216.

37. Lizzie Young was reportedly not in "robust health" but still maintained a busy work life in addition to being a "good housekeeper." Surveys of Indian Industry, 282319.

38. For example, John Roy, aged seventy-one, "hunts, traps, and fishes," his fifty-eight-year-old wife "makes moccasins and reed rugs," and "they pick and can wild berries and gather wild rice. This season they made 350 pounds of maple sugar and some syrup." The government reporter included making maple sugar and wild rice as part of the wife's household labor but probably understood that the couple traveled to the wild rice and sugar bush camps together. Surveys of Indian Industry, 282210.

39. Surveys of Indian Industry, 282215.

40. Ibid.

41. The Surveys of Indian Industry discussed approximately twenty women who were widowed, divorced, separated, or single adults at Lac du Flambeau.

42. Florina Denomie, "An Indian Huntress," Works Progress Administration: Chippewa Indian Historical Project Records, Envelope 7.

43. Charles E. Cleland, *The Place of the Pike (Gnoozhekaaning)* (Ann Arbor: University of Michigan Press, 2001), 31–48.

44. Kugel, *Main Leaders of Our People*, 124.

45. Michael McNally, *Ojibwe Singers: Hymns, Grief, and a Native Culture in Motion* (New York: Oxford University Press, 2000), 105.

46. Basil Johnston, *Ojibway Ceremonies* (Toronto: Bison Books, 1983).

47. Thomas Vennum, Jr., *The Ojibwa Dance Drum: Its History and Construction* (St. Paul: Minnesota Historical Society Press, 2009; originally published 1982), 82–83.

48. Frances Densmore, *Strength of the Earth: The Classic Guide to Ojibwe Uses of Native Plants* (St. Paul: Minnesota Historical Society Press, 2005; originally published 1928), 297.

49. Cleland, *Place of the Pike*, 60–61.

50. Their grandson, George Goggleye, related the story of their work to me in a conversation that took place June 15, 2008. He stated that his grandmother died in 1947 in Itasca County.

51. Child and White, "I've Done My Share," 197.

52. My mother told me this story when I was a girl, and I wrote about it in the introduction to a new edition to Frances Densmore's "Uses of Plants by the Chippewa Indians," published as *Strength of the Earth,* v–xi.

53. The story, like many Ojibwe stories, is often told without a strong reference to time and place. The interpretation that the jingle dress dance tradition emerged after the Spanish influenza pandemic is my own.

54. There is remarkably little literature on the history of the jingle dress. See Brenda J. Child, "Wilma's Jingle Dress: Ojibwe Women and Healing in the Early Twentieth Century," in *Reflections on American Indian History: Honoring the Past, Building a Future*, ed. Albert L. Hurtado (Norman: University of Oklahoma, 2008), 113–36.

4. NETT LAKE: *Wild Rice and the Great Depression*

1. The story of this Ojibwe family may be found in Brenda J. Child, *Boarding School Seasons: American Indian Families, 1900–1940* (Lincoln: University of Nebraska Press, 1998). Other histories of the American Indian boarding school experience include David W. Adams, *Education for Extinction: American Indians and the Boarding School Experience, 1875–1928* (Lawrence: University Press of Kansas, 1995); K. Tsianina Lomawaima, *They Called It Prairie Light: The Story of Chilocco Indian School* (Lincoln: University of Nebraska Press, 1994); Margaret Connell Szasz, *Education and the American Indian: The Road to Self-Determination Since 1928,* 2nd ed. (Albuquerque: University of New Mexico Press, 1977).

2. M. Inez Hilger, *Chippewa Families: A Social Study of White Earth Reservation* (St. Paul: Minnesota Historical Society Press, 1998; originally published 1938).

3. William Watts Folwell and Melissa Meyer documented the history of land fraud and dispossession the Ojibwe faced in Minnesota prior to the depression. William Watts Folwell, *A History of Minnesota,* Vol. IV (St. Paul: Minnesota Historical Society Press, 1930); Melissa Meyer, *The White Earth Tragedy: Ethnicity and Dispossession at a Minnesota Anishinaabe Reservation, 1889–1920* (Lincoln: Univeristy of Nebraska Press, 1994).

4. Federal Writers' Project of the Works Progress Administration, *The WPA Guide to Minnesota* (St. Paul: Minnesota Historical Society Press, 1985; originally published 1938), 38.

5. Ibid.

6. Most historians describe wild rice labor as shared by men and women. Brian C. Hosmer, *American Indians in the Marketplace: Persistence and Innovation Among the Menominees and Metlakatlans, 1870–1920* (Lawrence: University of Kansas Press, 1999), 22.

7. Frances Densmore, *Chippewa Customs* (St. Paul: Minnesota Historical Society Press, 1979; originally published 1929), 128.

8. Ibid.

9. Maude Kegg used the term *Oshkaabewisag* to refer to the ricing officials from Mille Lacs in Minnesota. Oshkaabewisag is the plural of a term that translates as "ceremonial attendant" or "messenger." Maude Kegg, *Portage Lake: Memories of an Ojibwe Childhood*, ed. John D. Nichols (Minneapolis: University of Minnesota Press, 1993), 122–23. Brian Hosmer mentions that the Menominee delegated a similar role to the warrior society, or *mitewuk*. Brian C. Hosmer, *American Indians in the Marketplace* (Lawrence: University of Kansas Press, 1999), 22. See also John D. Nichols and Earl Nyholm, *A Concise Dictionary of Minnesota Ojibwe* (Minneapolis: University of Minnesota Press, 1995).

10. Albert E. Jenks, "The Wild Rice Gatherers of the Upper Lakes: A Study in American Primitive Economics," *Nineteenth Annual Report of the Bureau of American Ethnology* 2 (1897–98).

11. Clark recalls that during his childhood, in the 1930s, his "parents" riced. Jim Clark, *Naawigiizis: The Memories of Center of the Moon*, ed. Louise Erdrich (Minneapolis: Birchbark Books Press, 2002), 62–64.

12. Thomas Vennum, Jr., *Wild Rice and the Ojibway People* (St. Paul: Minnesota Historical Society Press, 1988), 290.

13. Ibid., 290–96; Ray Larsen, "A Meander Through the Big Chip," *Wisconsin Department of Natural Resources Magazine* (October/November 1997).

14. Vennum, *Wild Rice and the Ojibway People*, 290–96.

15. The four-year cycle in wild rice production was the subject of a dissertation by Rachel Walker, "Wild Rice: The Dynamics of Its Population Cycles and the Debate over Its Control at the Minnesota Legislature" (Ph.D. diss., University of Minnesota, 2008).

16. Clark, *Naawigiizis*, 74–75.

17. Patricia Albers and William James suggest that as tourism grew in Minnesota, "the post card after 1920 lost much of its documentary role" and became "a photographic medium for tourists." Patricia C. Albers and William R. James, "Images and Reality: Post Cards of Minnesota's Ojibway People, 1900–80," *Minnesota History* 50, no. 1 (Summer 1985): 229–40.

18. Itasca State Park dates from 1891. The Douglas Lodge formally opened to visitors June 29, 1905, when Gov. John S. Johnson and his official party arrived at Itasca. The lodge was named for Wallace B. Douglas, a former

Minnesota attorney general and state Supreme Court member. "Douglas Lodge," Minnesota Department of Natural Resources.

19. "Indians in Minnesota Historical Pageants," *Indians at Work* (November 1, 1935).

20. The Minnesota Historical Society has photographs of the "Chippewa Village" at Itasca State Park and the "Indian Village" at the Minnesota State Fair.

21. Civilian Conservation Corps–Indian Division Handbook (March 1941).

22. Charles E. Cleland, *The Place of the Pike (Gnoozhekaaning)* (Ann Arbor: University of Michigan Press, 2001), 58–73.

23. National Archives and Records Administration, Record Group 75, Bureau of Indian Affairs, Kansas City Branch, Letters of the Consolidated Chippewa Agency, Series 164, Box 362.

24. Ibid., Series 212, Box 435.

25. Ibid., Series 164, Box 362.

26. Ibid.

27. George Morrison as told to Margot Fortunato Galt, *Turning the Feather Around: My Life in Art* (St. Paul: Minnesota Historical Society Press, 1998), 47.

28. IECW was the early name of the CCC-ID. News of Depression-era emergency conservation efforts was published from Washington in *Indians at Work* and regionally in Minnesota by the Consolidated Chippewa Agency in the *Chippewa Bulletin. Indians at Work* (February 15, 1934), 19–22.

29. Letters of the Consolidated Chippewa Agency, Series 207, Box 433.

30. Mustache said of the wild rice harvests, "Never see any women now." Quoted in Vennum, *Wild Rice and the Ojibway People*, 109–10.

31. Not all managers were non-Indian. The emergency work programs promoted an early employment policy of "Indian preference."

32. The photographs appeared in *Indians at Work* (November 15, 1934), 17. The pictures stand in contrast to Densmore's 1910 photographs in which women are paired as ricing partners.

33. Ibid., 23.

34. Sugar bush "improvement projects" followed. Washington slated educational programs at the plundered White Earth Reservation "for instruction of Indians in the proper method of tapping the maple trees," complaining that indigenous methods were "antiquated" because they did not make use of "wooden spouts" and other "modern methods." The Ojibwe were told, "If you want a steady income from your sugar bush use modern methods. Consult your extension agent for details." *Minnesota Chippewa Bulletin* (February 23, 1940). Gathering wild fruits was also

officially sanctioned when thirty boys and girls in the 4-H Club at Nett Lake were sent out to pick blueberries in the summer of 1939.

35. A 1942 report stated, "At present about one-third of the purchasers of wild rice licenses are of Indian blood." John B. Moyle, "Fisheries Research Investigational Report No 40, The 1941 Minnesota Wild Rice Crop," Bureau of Fisheries Research Division of Game and Fish, State of Minnesota, 39.

36. Charles E. Chambliss, "Wild Rice in Minnesota," National Archives and Records Administration, Records Group 75, Records of the Bureau of Indian Affairs, Central Plains Region, Kansas City, Missouri, Wild Rice Arts and Crafts Corporation, Series 138, Box 153.

37. The Indian Reorganization Act (IRA) of 1934, a major reform of the "Indian New Deal," remains controversial among scholars. At times they have pointed out how the federal legislation protected Indian rights, as Kenneth R. Philp wrote in *John Collier's Crusade for Indian Reform, 1920–1954* (Tucson: University of Arizona Press, 1977). Later authors have viewed the IRA more critically—for example, Thomas Biolsi, *Organizing the Lakota: The Political Economy of the New Deal on the Pine Ridge and Rosebud Reservation* (Tucson: University of Arizona Press, 1992).

38. *WPA Guide to Minnesota*, 38.

39. Ibid.

40. There were other buyers in addition to LaRoque appointed by the tribe. Six Ojibwe bands in Minnesota formed the Minnesota Chippewa Tribe in 1934. The Red Lake Reservation, where leaders wrote a tribal constitution in 1917, was not part of the MCT.

41. Wild Rice Arts and Crafts Corporation, November 22, 1938, Series 138, Box 151.

42. The bulk of the records left from the cooperative is correspondence, much of it letters to individuals who purchased wild rice.

43. Gedakaakoons is spelled Gidagaakoons and means "fawn" in the Minnesota Ojibwe dialect; *gidagaa-* refers to the spots, and *-koons* is diminutive, literally meaning "little spotted one."

44. Gedakaakoons and the Indian Maiden wear similar headbands, and the first Land O'Lakes Indian Maiden was pictured in a side pose. The Land O'Lakes corporate Web site details a short history of the Indian Maiden at http://landolakesinc.com/careers/whylandolakes/ecmd2-0016724.aspx.

45. "Summary, 1939 Portage Lake Wild Rice Project," Wild Rice Arts and Crafts Corporation, Series 138, Box 153. There were reported a dozen wild rice camps on Perch Lake in 1939.

46. Vennum, *Wild Rice and the Ojibway People*, 271.

47. For more on the resource management of the Great Lakes Indian Fish and Wildlife Commission, see http://www.glifwc.org.

5. MOUNT PLEASANT: *Metaphor of the Muskrat*

1. National Archives and Records Administration, Records Group 75, Records of the Bureau of Indian Affairs, Great Lakes Region, Chicago, Illinois, Records of the Mount Pleasant Indian School.

2. The standard works on the history of American Indian education include David W. Adams, *Education for Extinction: American Indians and the Boarding School Experience, 1875–1928* (Lawrence: University Press of Kansas, 1995); Brenda J. Child, *Boarding School Seasons: American Indian Families, 1900–1940* (Lincoln: University of Nebraska Press, 1998); K. Tsianina Lomawaima, *They Called It Prairie Light: The Story of Chilocco Indian School* (Lincoln: University of Nebraska Press, 1994).

3. National Archives and Records Administration, Records Group 75, Records of the Bureau of Indian Affairs, Great Lakes Region, Chicago, Illinois, Records of the Leech Lake Agency, April 6, 1900.

4. Basil H. Johnston, *Indian School Days* (Norman: University of Oklahoma Press, 1988), 21.

5. Charles E. Cleland, *The Place of the Pike (Gnoozhekaaning)* (Ann Arbor: University of Michigan Press, 2001), 42.

6. Ibid., 40.

7. Handbook of the U.S. Indian School Mt. Pleasant, Michigan, 1917–1918, Clarke Historical Library, Central Michigan University; Alice Littlefield, "Indian Education and the World of Work in Michigan, 1893–1933," in *Native Americans and Wage Labor: Ethnohistorical Perspectives*, eds. Alice Littlefield and Martha C. Knacks (Norman: University of Oklahoma Press, 1996).

8. John Bloom, *To Show What an Indian Can Do: Sports at Native American Boarding Schools* (Minneapolis: University of Minnesota Press, 2000).

9. Handbook of the U.S. Indian School Mt. Pleasant, Michigan, 1917-1918.

10. Ibid.

11. Records of the Mount Pleasant Indian School, February 24, 1933.

12. Ibid., Social Worker's Report, 1932.

13. Ibid., letter of February 24, 1933.

14. Child, *Boarding School Seasons*, 18–19.

15. National Archives and Records Administration, Records Group 75, Records of the Bureau of Indian Affairs, Central Plains Region, Kansas City, Missouri, Records of the Flandreau Indian School, letters June 1, July 9, July 11, 1925.

16. Ibid., letter February 4, 1938.

17. Child, *Boarding School Seasons*, Chapter 5, "Illness and Death"; and Diane Therese Putney, "Fighting the Scourge: American Indian Morbidity and Federal Policy, 1897–1928" (Ph.D. diss., Marquette University, 1980).

18. Child, *Boarding School Seasons*.
19. Records of the Flandreau Indian School, letter 1924.
20. Handbook of the U.S. Indian School Mt. Pleasant, Michigan, 1917–1918.
21. Ibid.
22. Child, *Boarding School Seasons*, Chapter 6, "Working for the School."
23. Johnston, *Indian School Days*.
24. Records of the Mount Pleasant Indian School, letter of December 11, 1929.
25. Records of the Flandreau Indian School, Matron's Report, July 20, 1933.
26. Records of the Mount Pleasant Indian School, June 22, 1933.
27. Ibid., letter of February 21, 1934.
28. Ibid., letter of May 18, 1934.
29. Michigan Humanities Council and Saginaw Chippewa Tribe, "School Days Remembered: The Mount Pleasant Indian School Reunion 1991," video recording.

6. MINNEAPOLIS: *A Renaissance of Spirit*

1. Ignatia Broker, *Night Flying Woman: An Ojibway Narrative* (St. Paul: Minnesota Historical Society Press, 1983), 5.
2. Russell Thornton, *American Indian Holocaust and Survival: A Population History since 1492* (Norman: University of Oklahoma Press, 1987); also see his essay "Population: PreContact to the Present" in *Encyclopedia of North American Indians*, ed. Frederick E. Hoxie (Boston: Houghton Mifflin, 1996), 500–502; Nancy Shoemaker, "The American Indian Recovery: Demography and the Family, 1900–1980" (Ph.D. diss., University of Minnesota, 1991).
3. The 2000 U.S. Census revealed a national Indian population that was 79 percent urban.
4. There are many well-known histories of federal policy and allotment, including Francis Paul Prucha, *The Great Father: The United States Government and the American Indians,* 2 Vols. (Lincoln: University of Nebraska Press, 1984).
5. Records of the Flandreau Indian School, letter of April 23, 1924.
6. "An urban elder remembers the early years of the Minneapolis Indian community," in Pauline Brunette, "The Minneapolis Urban Indian Community," *Hennepin County History* 49, no. 1 (Winter 1989–90): 4–15.
7. Amelia Jones Fairbanks personal interview by Brenda Child, October 7, 2001. My aunt Amelia generously took part in this interview, two months

before her death from cancer on December 10, 2001. Amelia was the oldest of my mother's siblings, born April 7, 1926.

8. Ibid.

9. Broker, 1–11.

10. Ibid., 3–4

11. Roberta Head McKenzie interview by Karissa White and Brenda Child, Minnesota's Greatest Generation Oral History Project, Minnesota Historical Society, July 24, 2006.

12. Ibid.

13. At the time of our 2006 interview, Roberta Head McKenzie was the oldest person attending the Red Lake Tribal College. McKenzie passed away in 2010.

14. Gertrude Howard Buckanaga interview by Brenda Child and Karissa White, Ojibwe Women Oral History Project, Minnesota Historical Society, August 10, 2007.

15. Ibid.

16. Sandra White Hawk, a Lakota activist on adoption issues, uses this term. Herself adopted by missionaries as a little girl on the Rosebud Reservation, she founded a program in Minnesota to reunite other adoptees with the Indian communities. In 2007, the White Earth Reservation became the first tribe in the country to offer an official, publicized "Welcome Home Gathering" to returning adoptees during the annual June powwow.

17. Dan Gunderson, "White Earth Nation Welcomes Adoptees Home," *Minnesota Public Radio*, October 5, 2007.

18. Suzanne Garner, "The Indian Child Welfare Act: A Review," *Wicazo Sa Review* 9, no. 1 (Spring 1993): 48.

19. Ibid., 47–51.

20. Rose Robinson interview by Brenda Child and Karissa White, Ojibwe Women Oral History Project, August 17, 2007.

21. Ibid.

22. Ibid.

23. Broker, *Night Flying Woman*, 6.

24. Also see *American Indian Quarterly* 2, nos. 3–4 (Summer–Fall 2003), a special issue edited by Susan Applegate Krouse and Heather Howard-Bobiwash, dedicated to American Indian women and their work in the Indian community of the United States and Canada.

25. Dennis Banks with Richard Erdoes, *Ojibwa Warrior: Dennis Banks and the Rise of the American Indian Movement* (Norman: University of Oklahoma Press, 2004), 61–63.

26. Paul Chaat Smith and Robert Allen Warrior, *Like a Hurricane* (New York: New Press, 1996).

27. Julie Davis, "American Indian Movement Survival Schools in Minneapolis and St. Paul, 1968–2002" (Ph.D. diss., Arizona State University, 2004), 101.

28. Vikki Howard interview by Brenda Child and Karissa White, Ojibwe Women Oral History Project, August 16, 2007.

29. Ibid.

30. Ibid.

31. Broker, *Night Flying Woman*, 5.

32. Daniel M. Cobb, *Native Activism in Cold War America: The Struggle for Sovereignty* (Lawrence: University of Kansas Press, 2008).

33. My view is similar to that of Krouse and Howard-Bobiwash in their study on urban women's roles in the Indian community of the United States and Canada (see n. 23).

34. Pat Bellanger interview by Brenda Child and Karissa White, Ojibwe Women Oral History Project, 2007.

BIBLIOGRAPHY

❦

MANUSCRIPT COLLECTIONS USED IN TEXT

Archives of the Franciscan Sisters of Perpetual Adoration, La Crosse, Wisconsin

Works Progress Administration, Chippewa Indian Historical Project

Minnesota Historical Society (MHS), St. Paul, Minnesota

Alexander Ramsey Papers
Emily Peake Papers
Julia A. Spears and Family Papers, 1839–1923
Minnesota's Greatest Generation Oral History Project
Ojibwe Women Oral History Project

National Archives and Records Administration (NARA), Record Group (RG) 75, Records of the Bureau of Indian Affairs (BIA), Central Plains Region, Kansas City, Missouri

Letters of the Consolidated Chippewa Agency
Records of the Flandreau Indian School
Wild Rice Arts and Crafts Records

National Archives and Records Administration (NARA), Records Group (RG) 75, Records of the Bureau of Indian Affairs (BIA), Great Lakes Region, Chicago, Illinois

Records of the Leech Lake Agency
Records of the Mount Pleasant Indian School
Surveys of Indian Industry, Lac du Flambeau Agency

State Historical Society of Wisconsin (SHSW), Ashland Area Research Center, Ashland, Wisconsin

Wisconsin Circuit Court, Washburn County Case Files, 1886–1982

ORAL HISTORIES

Published accounts of Ojibwe oral traditions in English and Ojibwemowin (the Ojibwe language) are important texts for both scholars as well as contemporary Ojibwe people engaged in cultural revitalization efforts in Ojibwe communities. As scholars seek to include more kinds of sources in their histories, oral traditions are increasingly important and provide another perspective apart from archival sources left by non-Indian government officials or traders. While most scholars and other observers of Ojibwe life in the nineteenth and early twentieth century did not attempt to preserve the stories they heard in the Ojibwe language, what was preserved contains a good breadth of traditions that scholars can utilize. Traditions regarding Ojibwe origins, labor, gender roles, politics, and treaties were recorded in the Ojibwe language. The recent work of linguists and other scholars has ensured that Ojibwe language sources are accessible for scholars and speakers of the Ojibwe language.

Benton-Banai, Edward. *The Mishomis Book: The Voice of the Ojibway.* St. Paul, MN: Red School House, 1988.

Jones, Dennis. "The Etymology of Anishinaabe." *Oshkaabewis Native Journal* 2:1 (Fall 1995): 43–48.

Jones, William. *Ojibwa Texts.* Truman Michelson, ed. New York: G. E. Steechert, 1917 & 1919.

Kegg, Maude. *Portage Lake: Memories of an Ojibwe Childhood.* John D. Nichols, ed. Minneapolis: University of Minnesota Press, 1993.

Nichols, John D., ed. *Statement Made by the Indians: A Bilingual Petition of the Chippewas of Lake Superior, 1864.* London, Ontario, Canada: University of Western Ontario, 1988.

Treuer, Anton. *Living Our Language: Ojibwe Tales and Oral Histories.* St. Paul: Minnesota Historical Society, 2001.

Treuer, Anton. "What's in a Name: The Meaning of Ojibwe." *Oshkaabewis Native Journal* 2:1 (Fall 1995): 39–41.

OJIBWE LANGUAGE DICTIONARIES

Father Frederic Baraga published the first Ojibwe language dictionary in 1878. The more recent dictionary of Nichols and Nyholm utilizes the Fiero orthography or double-vowel system of writing Ojibwe that is preferred by the vast majority of Ojibwe language educators. However, Baraga's pioneering work is still valuable, as it contains many older words not included in the Nichols and Nyholm dictionary, which focuses more on everyday usage of Ojibwe.

Baraga, Frederic. *A Dictionary of the Ojibway Language.* St. Paul: Minnesota Historical Society Press, 1992 (originally published 1878).

Nichols, John D., and Earl Nyholm. *A Concise Dictionary of Minnesota Ojibwe*. Minneapolis: University of Minnesota Press, 1995.

FUR TRADE

It is difficult to overstate the impact of the fur trade on Ojibwe history. The growth of Ojibwe communities from small areas in the Great Lakes to territories hundreds of miles south and west was due in large part to the dynamics of the fur trade. Consequently, Ojibwe communities often play large roles in histories of the fur trade. Over the last three decades, scholars have worked to broaden histories of the fur trade to include the role of women. Fur trade scholarship was profoundly affected by Richard White's *The Middle Ground* in 1991. White's ideas about the roles of exchange, understanding, and misunderstanding between the French and Algonquian peoples in creating a unique space in the Great Lakes have had a tremendous impact on the field and American history in general. Smaller case studies published since have utilized White's framework and expanded and critiqued White's ideas about life in the Great Lakes during the fur trade.

Bohaker, Heidi. "Nindoodemag: The Significance of Algonquian Kinship Networks in the Eastern Great Lakes Region, 1600–1701." *The William and Mary Quarterly* 63:1 (January 2006): 23–52.

Brown, Jennifer S. H. *Strangers in Blood: Fur Trade Company Families in Indian Country*. Vancouver: University of British Columbia Press, 1980.

Peterson, Jacqueline. "Prelude to Red River: A Social Portrait of the Great Lakes Metis." *Ethnohistory* 25:1 (Winter 1978): 41–67.

Peterson, Jacqueline, and Jennifer S. H. Brown, eds. *The New Peoples: Being and Becoming Metis in North America*. Winnipeg: University of Manitoba, 1985.

Schenck, Theresa M. *The Voice of the Crane Echoes Afar: The Sociopolitical Organization of the Lake Superior Ojibwa, 1640–1855*. New York: Garland, 1997.

Sleeper-Smith, Susan. *Indian Woman and French Men: Rethinking Cultural Encounter in the Western Great Lakes*. Amherst: University of Massachusetts, 2001.

Van Kirk, Sylvia. *Many Tender Ties: Women in Fur-Trade Society, 1670–1870*. Norman: University of Oklahoma Press, 1983.

White, Bruce. "A Skilled Game of Exchange: Ojibwe Fur Trade Protocol." *Minnesota History* 50:6 (Summer 1987): 229–240.

White, Bruce. "The Woman Who Married a Beaver: Trade Patterns and Gender Roles in the Ojibwa Fur Trade." *Ethnohistory* 46:1 (Winter 1999): 109–147.

White, Richard. *The Middle Ground: Indians, Empires, and Republics in the*

Great Lakes Region, 1650–1815. Cambridge: Cambridge University Press, 1991.

NINETEENTH-CENTURY ACCOUNTS

Accounts of Ojibwe life produced within the nineteenth century contain invaluable data about Ojibwe cultural, economic, social, and spiritual ways of the time. However, these oft-cited texts contain biases that modern readers must bear in mind. Nearly all the authors were directly involved in the process of American colonialism as either traders or government agents. All the authors were influenced by broader views of native people held by Euro-American society at the time. These views of native people as warlike and savage were linked to the process and provided justification for native dispossession occurring at the time. Nevertheless, these works are crucial to understanding Ojibwe life at a time when Ojibwe people were under immense pressure to change. Illustrating this dynamic perfectly is the foundational work to Ojibwe history: William Warren's *History of the Ojibway People.* A mixed-blood Ojibwe, Warren bore many of the biases held by Euro-Americans of the time. However, Warren's work is crucial to understanding Ojibwe history. Based on oral histories of his Ojibwe relatives and colleagues, much of the information Warren presented was not available anywhere before or since.

Armstrong, Benjamin G. *Early Life Among the Indians.* Ashland, WI: A. W. Bowron, 1892.

Blackbird, Andrew J. *History of the Ottawa and Chippewa Indians of Michigan; A Grammar of their Language, and Personal and Family History of the Author.* Ypsilanti, MI: The Ypsilantian Job Printing House, 1887.

Carver, Jonathan. *Carver's Travels in Wisconsin.* New York: Harper & Brothers, 1838.

Catlin, George. *Letters and Notes on the Manners, Customs, and Condition of the North American Indians.* Minneapolis: Ross & Haines, 1965 (originally published 1841).

Copway, George. *The Traditional History and Characteristic Sketches of the Ojibway Nation.* Boston: Sanbirn, Carter, Brazen & Co., 1850.

Enmegahbowh, John Johnson. *En-me-gah-bowh's Story: An Account of the Disturbances of the Chippewa Indians at Gull Lake in 1857, and Their Removal in 1868.* Minneapolis: Woman's Auxiliary St. Barnabas Hospital, 1904.

Gilfillan, Joseph A. "The Ojibways in Minnesota." *Collections of the Minnesota Historical Society* 9, 55–128.

Jones, Peter. *History of the Ojebway Indians; With Especial Reference to Their Conversion to Christianity.* London: A. W. Bennett, 1861.

Kohl, Johann Georg. *Kitchi-Gami: Life Among the Lake Superior Ojibway.* St.

Paul: Minnesota Historical Society Press, 1985 (originally published 1860).

McKenney, Thomas. *Sketches of a Tour to the Lakes*. Minneapolis: Ross & Haines, 1959 (originally published 1827).

Morse, Richard F. "The Chippewas of Lake Superior." *Collections of the State Historical Society of Wisconsin,* Vol. III. Lyman Copland Draper, ed. Madison: Wisconsin Historical Society, 1904, 338–69.

Nelson, George. *My First Years in the Fur Trade*. Theresa Schenck and Laura Peers, eds. St. Paul: Minnesota Historical Society, 2002.

Nicollet, Joseph N. *The Journals of Joseph N. Nicollet: A Scientist on the Mississippi Headwaters With Notes on Indian Life, 1837–1838*. St. Paul: Minnesota Historical Society, 1970.

Parker, Robert Dale, ed. *The Sound the Stars Make Rushing Through the Sky: The Writings of Jane Johnston Schoolcraft*. Philadelphia: University of Pennsylvania Press, 2007.

Pike, Zebulon Montgomery. *The Journals of Zebulon Montgomery Pike, with Letters and Related Documents*. Donald Jackson, ed. Norman: University of Oklahoma Press, 1966 (originally published 1810).

Schoolcraft, Henry R. *Personal Memoirs of a Residence of Thirty Years with the Indian Tribes on the American Frontiers*. Philadelphia: Lippincott, Grambo, and Co., 1851.

Schoolcraft, Henry R. *Schoolcraft's Expedition to Lake Itasca: The Discovery of the Source of the Mississippi*. East Lansing: Michigan State University, 1993 (originally published 1834).

Schoolcraft, Henry R. *Schoolcraft's Ojibwa Lodge Stories: Life on the Lake Superior Frontier*. Philip P. Mason, ed. East Lansing: Michigan State University Press, 1997 (originally published 1826 & 1827).

Schoolcraft, Henry R. *Summary Narrative of an Exploratory Expedition to the Sources of the Mississippi River, in 1820*. Philadelphia: Lippincott, Grambo, and Co., 1855.

Tanner, John. *The Falcon: A Narrative of the Captivity and Adventures of John Tanner*. New York: Penguin Books, 1994 (originally published 1830).

Warren, William W. *History of the Ojibwe People*. St. Paul: Minnesota Historical Society Press, 1984 (originally published 1885).

ANTHROPOLOGY

Much like their predecessors in the nineteenth century, twentieth-century anthropologists have left much valuable information while reflecting biases. Certain works (for example, Densmore's "The Native Art of the Chippewa" or Casagrande's "John Mink, Ojibwa Informant") lament losses of Ojibwe culture that reflect the times in which they were written and speak to the immense changes faced by early-twentieth-century Ojibwe people. Furthermore, anthropologists differed widely in their relationship with Ojibwe communities. Some were distant, detached observers, while others were actively involved in the lives of their "informants" beyond their professional relationship.

Barnouw, Victor. *Wisconsin Chippewa Myths & Tales and Their Relation to Chippewa Life.* Madison: University of Wisconsin Press, 1977.

Casagrande, Joseph. "John Mink, Ojibwa Informant," *Wisconsin Archaeologist* 36:4 (December 1955): 106–28.

Coleman, Sister Bernard. "The Ojibwa and the Wild Rice Problem." *Anthropological Quarterly* 26:3 (July 1943): 79–88.

Densmore, Frances. *Chippewa Customs.* St. Paul: Minnesota Historical Society, 1979 (originally published 1929).

Densmore, Frances. *Chippewa Music.* Minneapolis: Ross & Haines, 1973 (originally published 1910 & 1913).

Densmore, Frances. *Strength of the Earth: The Classic Guide to Ojibwe Uses of Native Plants.* St. Paul: Minnesota Historical Society Press, 2005 (originally published 1928).

Densmore, Frances. "The Native Art of the Chippewa." *American Anthropologist* 43:4 (October–December 1941): 678–81.

Hickerson, Harold. *The Chippewa and Their Neighbors: A Study in Ethnohistory.* Prospect Heights, IL: Waveland Press, 1988 (originally published 1970).

Hilger, Inez M. *Chippewa Child Life and Its Cultural Background.* St. Paul: Minnesota Historical Society Press, 1992 (originally published 1951).

Hilger, Inez M. *Chippewa Families: A Social Study of White Earth Reservation.* St. Paul: Minnesota Historical Society Press, 1998 (originally published 1938).

Jenks, Albert E. "The Wild Rice Gatherers of the Upper Lakes: A Study in American Primitive Economics." *Nineteenth Annual Report of the Bureau of American Ethnology* 2 (1897–98): 1013–1133.

Landes, Ruth. *Ojibwa Religion and the Midewiwin.* Madison: University of Wisconsin Press, 1968.

Landes, Ruth. *Ojibwa Sociology.* New York: Columbia University Press, 1937.

Landes, Ruth. *The Ojibwa Woman.* New York: Columbia University Press, 1938.

Ritzenthaler, Robert E., and Pat Ritzenthaler. *The Woodland Indians of the Western Great Lakes.* Prospect Heights, IL: Waveland Press, 1988 (originally published 1970).

Vennum, Thomas, Jr. "The Ojibwa Begging Dance." *Music and Context: Essays for John M. Ward.* Anne Dhu Shapiro, ed. Cambridge, MA: Harvard University Press, 1985.

Vennum, Thomas Jr. *The Ojibwa Dance Drum: Its History and Construction*. Washington, D.C.: Smithsonian Institution, 1982.

TWENTIETH-CENTURY OJIBWE WRITERS

While the works of such nineteenth-century Ojibwe writers as William Warren and Andrew Blackbird are extremely valuable historically, their work emphasized a Euro-American audience and sometimes echoed Euro-American stereotypes of native people. In addition, nineteenth-century Ojibwe writers tended to either be of mixed ancestry and claim a distinct identity from Ojibwe people (such as Warren or Jane Johnston Schoolcraft) or be recent converts to Christianity (such as Blackbird and Peter Jones), who favored the "progress" of Euro-American and Canadian "civilization." Accordingly, these works tended to emphasize the humanity of native people and argue against the outright extermination of native communities to Euro-American audiences. However, in the twentieth century Ojibwe voices emerged as a response to the assimilationist goals of Indian education. Thus, many Ojibwe writers in the twentieth century emphasized the value of traditional culture. The result was a much deeper engagement of issues important to Ojibwe people and a commitment to cultural revitalization that was directed toward both a native and non-native audience.

Broker, Ignatia. *Night Flying Woman: An Ojibway Narrative*. St. Paul: Minnesota Historical Society Press, 1983.

Clark, Jim. *Naawigiizis: Memories of Center of the Moon*. Louise Erdrich, ed. Minneapolis: Birchbark Books Press, 2002.

Johnston, Basil. *Indian School Days*. Toronto: Key Porter Books, 1988.

Johnston, Basil. *The Manitous: The Spiritual World of the Ojibway*. New York: HarperCollins Publishers, 1995.

Johnston, Basil. *Ojibway Ceremonies*. Toronto: McCleland & Stewart, 1982.

Johnston, Basil. *Ojibway Heritage*. Toronto: McCleland & Stewart, 1976.

Morriseau, Norval. *Legends of My People the Great Ojibway*. Selwyn Dewdney, ed. Toronto: Ryerson Press, 1965.

Morrison, Eliza. *A Little History of My Forest Life*. Austin J. McLean, ed. LaCrosse, WI: Sumac Press, 1978.

Morrison, George, as told to Margot Fotunato Galt. *Turning the Feather Around: My Life in Art*. St. Paul: Minnesota Historical Society Press, 1998.

Northrup, Jim. *The Rez Road Follies: Canoes, Casinos, Computers, and Birch Bark Baskets*. New York: Kodansha International, 1997.

Northrup, Jim. *Walking the Rez Road*. Stillwater, MN: Voyageur Press, 1993.

Rogers, John. *Red World and White: Memories of a Chippewa Boyhood*. Norman: University of Oklahoma Press, 1996 (originally published 1957).

Vizenor, Gerald, ed. *Anishenabe Adisokan: Tales of the People*. Minneapolis: Nodin Press, 1965.

Vizenor, Gerald, ed. *Anishenabe Nagomen: Songs of the People*. Minneapolis: Nodin Press, 1965.

Vizenor, Gerald. *Bear Island: The War at Sugar Point*. Minneapolis: University of Minnesota Press, 2006.

Vizenor, Gerald. *The Everlasting Sky: Voices of the Anishinabe People*. St. Paul: Minnesota Historical Society Press, 2000 (originally published 1972).

Vizenor, Gerald. *The People Named The Chippewa*. Minneapolis: University of Minnesota Press, 1984.

GENERAL HISTORICAL WORKS

Works on many Ojibwe communities attempt to find common themes in the histories while recognizing the sometimes vast economic, social, and cultural differences among Ojibwe communities. These works are organized around common experiences, such as political life (Kugel's *To Be the Main Leaders of Our People*), resources (Vennum's *Wild Rice and the Ojibway People*), or historical events (Clifton's "Wisconsin Death March"). These works also reflect changing scholarly attitudes about doing native history. Increasingly scholars have found native voices in archival sources, adding new dimensions to familiar histories.

Albers, Patricia C., and William James. "Images and Reality: Post Cards of Minnesota's Ojibway People, 1900-80." *Minnesota History* 50:1 (Summer 1985): 229–40.

Child, Brenda. *Boarding School Seasons: American Indian Families, 1900–1940*. Lincoln: University of Nebraska Press, 1998.

Child, Brenda. "Wilma's Jingle Dress: Ojibwe Women and Healing in the Early Twentieth Century." In *Reflections on American Indian History: Honoring the Past, Building a Future*. Albert L. Hurtado, ed. Norman: University of Oklahoma, 2008, pp. 113–36.

Cleland, Charles E. *Rites of Conquest: The History and Culture of Michigan's Native Americans*. Ann Arbor: University of Michigan Press, 1992.

Clifton, James. "Wisconsin Death March: Explaining the Extremes in Old Northwest Indian Removal." *Transactions of the Wisconsin Academy of Sciences, Arts and Letters* 75 (1987): 1–39.

Danziger, Edmund Jefferson. *The Chippewas of Lake Superior*. Norman: University of Oklahoma Press, 1979.

Konkle, Maureen. *Writing Indian Nations: Native Intellectuals and the Politics of Historiography, 1827–1863*. Chapel Hill: University of North Carolina Press, 2004.

Kugel, Rebecca. *To Be the Main Leaders of Our People: A History of Minnesota Ojibwe Politics, 1825–1898*. Lansing: Michigan State University, 1998.

Littlefield, Alice. "Indian Education and the World of Work in Michigan, 1893–1933." In *Native Americans and Wage Labor: Ethnohistorical Perspectives,* Alice Littlefield and Martha C. Knacks, eds. Norman: University of Oklahoma Press, 1996.

Oberly, James W. "Land, Population, Prices, and the Regulation of Natural Resources: The Lake Superior Ojibwa, 1790–1920." In *The Other Side of the Frontier: Economic Explorations into Native American History.* Linda Barrington, ed. Boulder, CO: Westview Press, 1999.

Peacock, Thomas, and Marlene Wisuri. *Ojibwe Waasa Inaabidaa.* Afton, MN: Afton Historical Society Press, 2001.

Rasmussen, Charlie Otto. *Ojibwe Journeys: Treaties, Sandy Lake & the Waabanong Run.* Odanah, WI: Great Lakes Indian Fish and Wildlife Commission, 2003.

Schenck, Theresa M. "William W. Warren's History of the Ojibway People: Tradition, History, and Context." In *Reading Beyond Words: Contexts for Native History,* Jennifer S. H. Brown and Elizabeth Vibert, eds. Peterborough, Ontario: Broadview Press, 2003, pp. 193–210.

Schenck, Theresa M. *William W. Warren: The Life, Letters, and Times of an Ojibwe Leader.* Lincoln: University of Nebraska, 2007.

Tanner, Helen Hornbeck. *Atlas of Great Lakes Indian History.* Norman: University of Oklahoma Press, 1987.

Tanner, Helen Hornbeck. *The Ojibwas: A Critical Bibliography.* Bloomington: Indiana University Press, 1976.

Vennum, Thomas Jr. *Wild Rice and the Ojibway People.* St. Paul: Minnesota Historical Society, 1988.

COMMUNITY HISTORIES

Histories of Ojibwe communities vary widely despite the fact that all of the studies below were produced in the past twenty-five years. Some reflect community desires to see their stories known (Peacock, *A Forever Story*) while others attempt to contextualize the histories of Ojibwe communities within the framework of Indian history or American history more broadly (Meyer, *The White Earth Tragedy*). Regardless, there is a need for histories of Ojibwe communities within both of these categories. Each Ojibwe community has a unique story that needs to be heard. This is especially evident when one considers the vast territory inhabited by Ojibwe people. Most Ojibwe communities have little published literature on their history, and what has been published is usually scattered over a variety of sources. The incentive for scholars is two-fold: opportunities to help Ojibwe people better understand their history and to expand the existing narrative of American Indian history.

Beaulieu, David. "Curly Hair and Big Feet: Physical Anthropology and Implementation of Land Allotment on the White Earth Chippewa Reservation." *American Indian Quarterly* 8:4 (Fall 1984): 281–314.

Birmingham, Robert A. "Dogtown: A Historical and Archeological Study of a Late Historic St. Croix Chippewa Community." *The Wisconsin Archeologist* 65:3 (September 1984): 183–300.

Burt, Larry. "Nowhere Left to Go: Montana's Crees, Metis and Chippewas and the Creation of Rocky Boy's Reservation." *Great Plains Quarterly* 7 (Summer 1987): 195–209.

Camp, Gregory S. "Working Out Their Own Salvation: The Allotment of Land in Severalty and the Turtle Mountain Chippewa Band, 1870–1920." *American Indian Culture and Research Journal* 14:2 (Spring 1990): 19–38.

Cleland, Charles E. *The Place of the Pike (Gnoozhekaaning): A History of the Bay Mills Indian Community*. Ann Arbor: University of Michigan Press, 2001.

Coleman, Sister Bernard. *Where the Water Stops: Fond du Lac Reservation*. Duluth, MN: College of St. Scholastica, 1967.

Doherty, Robert. "Old-Time Origins of Modern Sovereignty: State-Building among the Keeweenaw Bay Ojibway, 1832–1854." *American Indian Quarterly* 31:1 (Winter 2007): 166–87.

McClurken, James M., ed. *Fish in the Lakes, Wild Rice, and Game in Abundance: Testimony on Behalf of Mille Lacs Ojibwe Hunting and Fishing Rights*. East Lansing: Michigan State University Press, 2000.

Magelssen, Scott. "Remapping American-ness: Heritage Production and the Staging of the Native American and the African American as Other in 'Historyland.'" *National Identities* 4:2 (July 2002): 161–78.

Meyer, Melissa L. *The White Earth Tragedy: Ethnicity and Dispossession at a Minnesota Anishinaabe Reservation, 1889–1920*. Lincoln: University of Nebraska, 1994.

The Minnesota Chippewa Tribe. *White Earth: A History*. Cass Lake, MN: Minnesota Chippewa Tribe, 1989.

Mittelholtz, Erwin F. *Historical Review of the Red Lake Indian Reservation: A History of Its People and Progress*. Bemidji: Beltrami County Historical Society, 1957.

Nesper, Larry. "Simulating Culture: Being Indian for the Tourists in Lac du Flambeaus Wa-Swas-Gon Indian Bowl." *Ethnohistory* 50:3 (Summer 2003): 447–72.

Oberly, James W. "Tribal Sovereignty and Natural Resources: The Lac Courte Oreilles Experience." In *Buried Roots and Indestructible Seeds: The Survival of American Indian Life in Story, History, and Spirit,* Mark A. Linquist and Martin Zanger, eds. Madison: University of Wisconsin, 1994, pp. 127–153.

Peacock, Thomas, ed. *A Forever Story: The People and Community of the Fond du Lac Reservation*. Cloquet, MN: Fond du Lac Band of Lake Superior Chippewa, 1998.

Rasmussen, Charlie Otto. *Where the River Is Wide: Pahquahwong and the Chippewa Flowage*. Odanah, WI: Great Lakes Indian Fish and Wildlife Commission, 1998.

Ross, Hamilton Nelson. *La Pointe, Village Outpost*. St. Paul, MN: North Central Publishing, 1960.

Youngbear-Tibbetts, Holly. "Without Due Process: The Alienation of Individual Trust Allotments of the White Earth Anishinaabeg." *American Indian Culture and Research Journal* 15:2 (Spring 1991): 93–138.

WISCONSIN

Many scholars convincingly demonstrate that Wisconsin is an important state in the study of American Indian history due to the diverse historical experiences among the state's tribes. Several important themes of American Indian history such as growth of small tribes into major powers during the fur trade, the effect of removed tribes on tribes from the area, the effectiveness of armed resistance, the impact of allotment, and termination are central to the histories of Wisconsin's tribes. Six of the eleven federally recognized tribes in Wisconsin are Ojibwe communities. While the diversity of Wisconsin's tribes has brought much scholarly attention, Wisconsin Ojibwe are typically at the center of these stories.

Bieder, Robert E. *Native American Communities in Wisconsin, 1600–1960: A Study of Tradition and Change*. Madison: University of Wisconsin, 1995.

Godfrey, Anthony. *A Forest History of Ten Wisconsin Indian Reservations Under the Great Lakes Agency: Precontact to the Present*. Salt Lake City: U.S. West Research, 1996.

Loew, Patty. *Indian Nations of Wisconsin: Histories of Endurance and Renewal*. Madison: Wisconsin Historical Society Press, 2001.

Loew, Patty. "Native, Newspapers, and 'Fighting Bob': Wisconsin Chippewa in the 'Unprogressive' Era." *Journalism History* 23:4 (Winter 1997–98): 149–59.

Loew, Patty. "Tinker to Evers to Chief: Baseball from Indian Country." *Wisconsin Magazine of History* 87:3 (Spring 2004): 2–13.

Lurie, Nancy Oestreich. *Wisconsin Indians*. Madison: Wisconsin Historical Society Press, 2002.

Pfaff, Tim. *Paths of the People: The Ojibwe in the Chippewa Valley*. Eau Claire: Chippewa Valley Museum, 1993.

CANADA

The studies of Canadian Ojibwe communities make clear the distinction between them and Ojibwe communities in the United States. The work of the authors below emphasize the role Canadian Indian policy played in dispossessing Canadian Ojibwe from their lands and resources that are distinct and familiar to Ojibwe communities in the United States. Furthermore, the presence of numerous Ojibwe communities on the Canadian Plains contrasts with more woodland-based U.S. Ojibwe communities. Studies of Plains Ojibwe or Saulteaux communities make clear that Ojibwe people adapted to the vast differences of landscape on the Plains while maintaining Ojibwe culture and traditions.

Borrows, John. *Recovering Canada: The Resurgence of Indigenous Law.* Toronto: University of Toronto, 2002.

Holzkamm, Tim E., Leo G. Waisberg, and Joan A. Lovisek. "'Stout Athletic Fellows': The Ojibwa During the 'Big Game Collapse' in Northwestern Ontario 1821–1871." In *Papers of the 26th Algonquian Conference, University of Manitoba, Winnepeg,* 1995, pp. 169–82.

Kinew, Kathy Avery. "Manito Gitigaan: Governance in the Great Spirit's Garden Wild Rice in Treaty #3 from Pre-Treaty to the 1990s." In *Papers of the 26th Algonquian Conference,* University of Manitoba, Winnepeg, 1995, pp. 183–94.

Leighton, Douglas. "The Manitoulin Incident of 1863: An Indian-White Confrontation." *Ontario History* 69:2 (June 1977): 113–24.

Lovisek Joan A., Leo G. Waisberg, and Tim E. Holzkamm. "'Cultural Leprosy': The 'Aboriginal Ethnology' of Ruth Landes." In *Papers of the 27th Algonquian Conference,* University of Manitoba, Winnepeg, 1996, pp. 164–79.

Lovisek Joan A., Leo G. Waisberg, and Tim E. Holzkamm. "'Deprived of That Part of Their Living': Colonialism and Nineteenth Century Flooding of Ojibwa Lands." In *Papers of the 26th Algonquian Conference,* University of Manitoba, Winnepeg, 1995, pp. 226–39.

Peers, Laura. *The Ojibwa of Western Canada, 1780 to 1870.* St. Paul : Minnesota Historical Society Press, 1994.

Waisberg, Leo G., and Tim E. Holzkamm. "'A Tendency to Discourage Them From Cultivating': Ojibwa Agriculture and Indian Affairs Administration in Northwestern Ontario." *Ethnohistory* 40:2 (Spring 1993): 175–211.

Waisberg, Leo G., Joan A. Lovisek, and Tim E. Holzkamm. "Ojibwa Reservations as 'An Incubus upon the Territory': The Indian Removal Policy 1874–1982." In *Papers of the 27th Algonquian Conference,* University of Manitoba, Winnepeg, 1996, pp. 337–52.

TREATY RIGHTS

The struggle for Ojibwe people in Wisconsin, Upper Michigan, and eastern Minnesota to practice their off-reservation treaty rights garnered much attention in the 1980s. Violent confrontations at Wisconsin boat landings over Ojibwe spearfishing caught the attention of the national news media. Scholarly works have attempted to historicize the conflict and bring attention to vast efforts made by the states of Wisconsin, Michigan, and Minnesota in suppressing these rights for over one hundred years. At the same time, these authors stress that the contemporary practice of Ojibwe off-reservation rights goes beyond spearfishing to maple sugaring, gathering forest products, wild ricing, and hunting. As these works make clear, the fight to practice these rights and the actual practice of them are crucial to Ojibwe sovereignty.

Keller, Robert H. "Americas Native Sweet: Chippewa Treaties and the Right to Harvest Maple Sugar." *American Indian Quarterly* 11:2 (Spring 1989): 117–35.

Nesper, Larry. *The Walleye War: The Struggle for Ojibwe Spearfishing and Treaty Rights.* Lincoln: University of Nebraska Press, 2002.

Satz, Ronald N. *Chippewa Treaty Rights: The Reserve Rights of Wisconsin's Chippewa Indians in Historical Perspective.* Transactions of the Wisconsin Academy of Sciences, Arts and Letters Vol. 79, 1991.

Silvern, Steven. "Reclaiming the Reservation: The Geopolitics of Wisconsin Anishinaabe Resource Rights." *American Indian Research and Culture Journal* 24:3 (Fall 2000): 131–53.

Whaley, Rick, with Walter Bresette. *Walleye Warriors: An Effective Alliance Against Racism and for the Earth.* Philadelphia: New Society, 1994.

Wrone, David R. "The Economic Impact of the 1837 and 1842 Chippewa Treaties." *American Indian Quarterly* 17:3 (Summer 1993): 329–40.

WORLD WAR II, URBANIZATION, AND ACTIVISM

The massive urbanization of native people in the mid-twentieth century in the years before and after World War II was a major event in American Indian history. By 1970, the majority of native people nationally lived off reservations. This urbanization trend was aided by shifts in federal Indian policy following World War II. In the 1950s, while no Ojibwe communities were formally terminated, Ojibwe people were affected by the BIA's relocation program, which intentionally sought to relocate native peoples to cities. By the 1960s, cities in the Great Lakes such as Minneapolis–St. Paul, Milwaukee, Chicago, Toronto, Thunder Bay, and others had a sizable Ojibwe population. Like native people nationally, Ojibwe people faced numerous challenges adjusting to city life that directly led to activism. Ojibwe people were central to the leadership and membership of the Minneapolis-based American Indian Movement (AIM). AIM had a vast influence on Ojibwe people that went beyond its members or protests. Furthermore, AIM aided Ojibwe communities and tribal councils in struggles in the 1970s, such as the 1973 takeover of the Winter Dam at Lac Courte Oreilles. However, AIM was an organization fraught with contradictions and controversies. For example, in "Dennis of Wounded Knee," Ojibwe author Gerald Vizenor argues that some in AIM's leadership had views of women that were not in accordance with traditional Ojibwe values.

Banks, Dennis, with Richard Erdoes. *Ojibwa Warrior: Dennis Banks and the Rise of the American Indian Movement*. Norman : University of Oklahoma Press, 2004.

Loew, Patty. "The Back of the Homefront: Black and American Indian Women in Wisconsin During World War II." *Wisconsin Magazine of History* 82:2 (Winter 1998–1999): 82–103.

Smith, Paul Chaat, and Robert Allen Warrior. *Like a Hurricane: The Indian Movement from Alcatraz to Wounded Knee*. New York: The New Press, 1996.

Vizenor, Gerald. "Dennis of Wounded Knee." In *The People Named the Chippewa*. Minneapolis: University of Minnesota Press, 1984, pp. 124–38.

INDEX